Dynamics of Small Town Ministry

Lawrence W. Farris

Foreword by Norma Cook Everist

An Alban Institute Publication

Library of Congress Card Number 99-69583

ISBN 1-56699-228-1

In honor of
The Reverend Winslow Drummond Shaw
Skilled mentor, esteemed colleague, cherished friend

CONTENTS

ACKNOWLEDGMENTS

I am most grateful to the congregation of the First Presbyterian Church of Three Rivers–Centreville, Michigan, for calling me ten years ago to serve in a rather remarkable small town. Members' patience and responsiveness as I learned about the special character of small-town ministry was but one of many faithful responses to the grace of God. The saints of this congregation have a rare combination of faithfulness to their fine traditions and openness to the tasks to which God may yet call them in their shared life. They have been a source of great delight to me.

The many colleagues across several denominations with whom I have shared the challenges, joys, and frustrations of the small-community context have blessed me by the witness of their commitment to the church in what are often seen as out-of-the-way, even ignorable, places. Their companionship and creativity have been a source of strength and new possibility on many a day. Among this company, I am particularly grateful to the Rev. Alice Fleming Townley for her joyful and profound faith, and for her "older than her years" wisdom about creating church and loving God's people where they are.

I extend my gratitude to the Rev. Jim Kinsey of the Church of the Brethren of Lake Odessa, Michigan, for graciously lending me a number of helpful books and for his wise and good-humored comments on small-town ministry. I also appreciate the considerable efforts of the Three Rivers Public Library staff in tracking down needed reference materials. Jennifer Tice and Linda Hilton exemplified, through their generous help, much that is good about small towns. My gratitude is offered also to Western Michigan University's Waldo Library for extending privileges to anyone living within 50 miles of the facility. This enlightened policy is a great benefit to those of us living in the many small towns within that radius.

I am also grateful to the Alban Institute for giving me the opportunity to write about ministry in the small community—an area of the church's life too often overlooked. Out of his professional acumen and background as a once-upon-a-time small-town resident, editor David Lott has offered many wise and constructive suggestions that have enabled me to broaden my understanding of small communities.

My family members are more than blessings to me: They are grace-bearers. Patient with the time and energy writing takes, encouraging when I have gotten stuck, playful when I have become too serious, my wife Pat, son Jordan, and daughter Rachel again and again mirror the light of God's love into my life. They teach me how all things intermingle for good and for God for those who love God and one another.

FOREWORD

Whenever I see a television advertisement depicting life in the United States, I ask myself, "Is this for people in small towns or (seemingly) about them?" It's not hard to tell the difference. The latter is aimed at the urban market—which is vast. It portrays an idyllic, quaint small town. One can count the stereotypes and caricatures: old men passing time playing checkers, farm wives gathering eggs in a basket, no modern technology, no awareness of the outside world. This is not a small town I have ever seen. The other advertisement is for people who live in rural and small-town America. It portrays sophisticated agricultural procedures, the latest computer systems, global commodities markets, communal interdependence.

This book is no caricature. Lawrence Farris leads us into real places, into an understanding and appreciation that are neither romantic nor cynical. He provides both principles and practices for small-town ministry, where life is complex yet comprehensible. Often ministers enter small towns as outsiders. Farris helps us see how that vantage point need not hinder but can help provide perspective for leadership, if one takes the time to respect the people and to gain their trust. That's not a bad rubric for ministerial leadership anywhere.

More than demographics, we shall learn about self-image and a sense of worth. As I travel around the country visiting congregations, I'm frequently met at the door with the self-description, "We're not the church we used to be." I respond, "Then who are you?" No apologies needed. As I walk with people through their communities, I hear stories of individual and communal identity. *Dynamics of Small Town Ministry* helps us listen to and interpret those conversations.

People who live in the small towns to which we are called are already in ministry and probably have been for many years. The common care they show for one another they may not name "ministry," but it is. They may even describe themselves with seemingly self-deprecating wry humor. Once a longtime resident showed me around his community as I took pictures. We strolled each block but still found ourselves rather quickly back at the church. "Well, that's it," he said, "and you probably even have some film left." When I learn to listen in the local language, I hear people talking about their church with affection and amazing accuracy. Deep down, they know who they are and the role of their church in the social fabric.

People change everywhere. The God of steadfast love can sustain congregations and their communities amid uncertainty and fear. Such congregations are not alone but part of the historic and global church. We need to minister from that viewpoint. In these chapters Farris helps us ask about the nature of change, and the resistance to change so that we can minister effectively, leading people in their call to mission.

The book is full of questions, inviting us to "read the books" that are the people of God in the places we are called to serve. Each community has a unique history and a specific challenge. Many towns are becoming smaller; some are growing—or growing again. Urban Americans are realizing that in a computer age people can do business from anywhere. The small town of 2,000 in which I live is three-and-a-half hours by car from Chicago, but just a stroke of a computer key away. Why not live here? No place is isolated unless one wishes it to be so. The challenge may come in the different images of residents: those who have lived here for a long time, fully aware of the complexities and their connection to the wider world, and those who wish to escape urban life, believing they are moving to that idyllic image of the advertisement.

People living in small towns probably know a lot more about urban America than urban America knows about small towns. If you are reading this book because you are involved, or about to become involved, in small-town ministry, I suggest that you also share it with an urban colleague to read. Urban Americans need to learn.

Some ministers hesitate to move to a small town because they fear a lack of privacy. Farris acknowledges that reality: You may want to leave town to have a day off. But there's an irony here. In a nation that virtually worships individual independence and the resulting anonymity, people still hunger to be known, to be part of a community of shared values and meaning. Knowing someone's name and being known are important. Ministering in the name of the God who calls us by name in baptism calls us to learn people's names (even the people in the cemetery, Farris points out). In so doing we will be known—and trusted.

This book, written in an easy style, takes us into small-town life quietly and carefully, with courage and commitment. The author is not unaware of the challenges small towns face, including his own experience with hate groups that tried and failed to find fertile ground in his community. Farris writes out of his own many years of ministry in small towns, but he does not limit himself to personal experience. We each bring our own images, experiences, and viewpoints to ministry. Farris helps us see beyond, something that our ministry ought to help small-town congregations do.

The first part of this book helps us gain understanding, respect, and appreciation for small-town life in community. The second half provides compelling insights for small-town ministry: about longevity, insularity, and "homecoming." Farris reminds us that people may not be as provincial as they appear. His section on the ministry of forbearance is poignant and powerful.

Lawrence Farris invites us to bring ourselves and our backgrounds to small towns and to be prepared to learn, to grow, and to engage in sustainable ministry with people who faithfully live there. He provides creative, assertive possibilities for change and some refreshing leadership roles as trusted outsider, bridge builder, and community developer. He helps us learn how to learn from the people and how to help them grow— not necessarily in numbers, but in appreciation of God's grace among them.

NORMA COOK EVERIST
Wartburg Theological Seminary
Dubuque, Iowa

INTRODUCTION

Jesus went about all the cities and villages, teaching in their synagogues and preaching the gospel of the kingdom, and healing every disease and every infirmity (Matt. 9:35).

It has been my habit for some time to ask small-town residents just what they think makes a small town.

"It has to have a Main Street."

"A restaurant where the same folks have coffee every morning."

"You know you're in a small town if most everybody waves at you."

"It's usually at least five miles to the next one."

"You've heard what they say: 'There's not much to see, but what you hear more than makes up for it.' That's about it."

"There are lots of people around to tell you how it used to be. And how much better it used to be."

"The smallest ones have only a bar and a church. But they used to have a post office, a school, a general store, and a bank. And the train and bus both came through."

"Everybody knows everybody. And their parents and grandparents, too."

"People are open and friendly in small towns. You can be different and still belong."

"Small towns are getting more and more like everywhere else."

"People love their high-school sports in small towns."

"You can cash a check almost anywhere without ever having to show identification."

There is truth in all those assessments, both positive and negative. They are all part of why I have found ten years of small-town ministry enriching and rewarding. Life in a small town has led me to a spirituality and practice of ministry grounded in place and history, as well as to a confrontation with mass culture and economics breaking in upon small communities. As contexts for ministry, they are distinctly different from urban and suburban settings. In working with a variety of small-town pastors, I have found considerable variety among their communities. Said one Matthew Fair over a century ago: "I know no town like another, if it be truly known."[1] Contradictory attitudes on the part of outsiders toward small towns are also found within the hearts of small-town dwellers themselves. Small towns cannot be understood simply as either the stultifying Gopher Prairie of Sinclair Lewis's *Main Street* or the place-where-things-always-work-out of Jan Karon's hugely popular Mitford novels. It is their complexity that makes small-town ministry interesting and challenging. My purpose here is to delineate crucial characteristics of small towns and to explore practical aspects of ministry in such a context. Understanding these elements will make for more effective ministry.

It often becomes apparent to pastors new to small-town ministry that much of their seminary education has been biased toward a suburban or urban context. They often do not know what they are getting into or how to begin to comprehend it. Many books on ministry also assume, either explicitly or implicitly, that the context for ministry is urban or suburban. After all, cities and suburbs are where most people live, and that is where churches seem most likely to be gaining members or ministries. Denominations, although many of their churches are in small towns, may not always attend well to such churches. Says poet-essayist Kathleen Norris of her church in Lemmon, South Dakota:

> Perhaps it's not surprising that so tiny a rural congregation is not often well served by the larger church. . . . For all their pious talk of "small is beautiful," church bureaucrats, like bureaucrats everywhere, concentrate their attention on places with better demographics; bigger numbers, more power and money.[2]

Values and issues different from those of the cities and suburbs shape small-town ministry. Urban and suburban strategies for ministry may not translate easily into the small-town context. For example, techniques for assimilating new members in a suburban church where people are frequently moving to town or leaving, and newcomers are common, may not fit the small-town ethos, where mobility is lower and residents may be somewhat cautious about including newcomers at a level deeper than that dictated by common hospitality. Specific attention needs to be given to the particular nature of the small-town context.

Because almost 17,000 communities in the United States have a population under 10,000 (understood here as a small town),[3] small-town churches are numerous. At least 115,000 congregations are located in nonmetropolitan counties, and, by some estimates, perhaps as many as 200,000. In some denominations (e.g., Assemblies of God, AME Zion, Nazarene, Episcopal, Roman Catholic, Southern Baptist), the number of small-town churches has increased in recent years.[4] Some small towns, particularly those of relative ethnic homogeneity, may have few churches, while other towns may have many, to the point of being "overchurched," owing to ethnic or class diversity, or to a history of church conflicts. I had described to me recently a town of 5,000 boasting seven Baptist churches "all related by schism." And it should be noted that the churches of small towns may be small, large, or in between.

Statistically, small towns are growing. In the past 25 years, both the numbers of small towns and the number of people living in them have increased slightly.[5] As would be expected, the increase is not uniform across the country. The farm crisis of the 1980s meant a "massive shift of population from the countryside"[6] in some agricultural regions. But that decline has reversed.

> The revival of growth in rural American is one of the biggest demographic stories of the 1990s. Three in four nonmetropolitan counties gained population between 1990 and 1994, a stunning reversal following a decade of decline. Now the pace of rural growth seems to be accelerating.[7]

It has been further noted that even farming- and mining-dependent areas are growing with migration into rural areas, and it has been suggested that this growth

> is rooted in long-term economic changes . . . along with the conviction of many Americans that small town life is better than big city life. . . . It now appears that the rural hard times of the 1980s were only a brief reversal of a fundamental population shift. . . .

The rural rebound of the 1990s is fueled . . . by more rural residents staying put and some metropolitan residents moving to small towns and rural homes. Specifically, 56 percent [of the observed growth]. . . came from net gains in migration.[8]

What these small-town newcomers seek "is a piece of the simple life: friendly, slow-paced, basic, safe, a return to community on a human scale."[9] Those able to work out of their homes via computer, retirees no longer engaged in making a living, lower-income people seeking affordable housing, employees of the larger retail chains now opening in small towns, people willing to trade a longer commute for what is perceived as a better quality of life may all be candidates for migration away from urban and suburban communities.

But it is naïve to think of small towns as uncomplicated places in which to enjoy the simple and better life of a bygone era. It is true that in a world of rapid, multidirectional movement in every area of life, small towns can teach a great deal about permanence; and in a time of orientation toward and anxiety about the future, they can teach the value of history. But small towns also show considerable diversity. "There are so many kinds of towns— river towns, railroad towns, mill towns, market towns, company towns, cow towns, coal towns, college towns—and the differences are profound."[10] And small towns are complicated. Life there

is sometimes visualized as simple, with few interpersonal demands creating stress . . . [S]uch a perspective may be disappointed to learn that stress can come from needing to master the details [of] remembering not only customers' names, but those of their family, and even the year and model of their tractor.[11]

Finally, the ambivalent attitude of Americans toward small towns needs to be noted. "In American literature and drama, indeed through so much of our culture, two themes prevail concerning the small town—that it is close to ideal and that it is insufferable."[12] Small towns can be unhurried and quiet, keeping commonsense folk close to the natural world as well as dull, provincial, lacking in culture and charm, full of people afraid of the larger world—at the same time, in the same place.[13] Indeed, small-town residents themselves are torn between the effective traditions of the past and the changes required to survive in the future; between needing newcomers and fearing they will change what is cherished; between individual freedom and the treasured sense of belonging. Neither an excessively romantic nor a cynical view of small towns will well serve those who seek to minister in them. But an honest and appreciative understanding can be the foundation for a fulfilling ministry in the small town.

The lessons of modernity will no doubt be debated long into this new millennium. One lesson that seems clear, however, is the importance of understanding context in order to take effective action. Different contexts require different approaches. No "one style fits all" approach to ministry is applicable everywhere. This consideration of small towns and small-town ministry seeks to exegete the small-town context and to distinguish that context from its urban and suburban counterparts. It is offered in two parts. In Part I, "Discovering the Small Town," the role of geography and history in shaping a small town's present reality will be considered. Types of small towns as well as crucial aspects of their culture, values, and rhythms of life will be discussed. In Part II, "Ministering in the Small Town," the implications of Part I will be elucidated for such aspects of small-town work as ministerial role, pastoral care, and congregational role and ministry.

Discovering the Small Town

CHAPTER 1

Geography

In approaching ministry in a small town, some pastors may believe the best way to begin is first to get to know the congregation to be served, and then to move out into exploration of the community. While that assumption is perfectly understandable, let me suggest that it is better to begin with the town rather than the congregation. This is so because "small-town culture is like a map deeply embedded in the cognitive structure of those who have lived in it."[1] Understanding the community, learning the internal map its members carry, will take a minister a long way toward understanding the congregation.

> Although human beings have an insatiable yearning to shape space and live within built environments, they are still influenced by the places they create and natural forces they will never transcend.[2]

It is important first to answer two questions. What kind of small town is this? And what is the impact of its geographical setting?

Types of Small Towns

R. Alex Sim provides a helpful way of answering the first question by dividing small towns into four types: Ribbonvilles, Agravilles, Mighthavebeenvilles, and Fairviews.[3] A Ribbonville town was once a separate entity that is becoming increasingly drawn into a city's sphere of influence. Usually this integration is caused by urban sprawl, often following highways leading out from, or encircling, the urban center. Ribbonvilles are those small towns beginning to be converted into bedroom communities. Farmland may be subdivided; population and tax base may increase, often rapidly; mass culture in the form of a strip mall may already be present; and community orientation increasingly turns outward toward relationship with the encroaching urban area. Churches here are confronted with a change of identity; the incorporation of newcomers; and the presence of new, perhaps competing, congregations.

What Sim terms "Agravilles" are small towns somewhat further from cities; they function as service centers for a local economy, perhaps based in agriculture, mining, or forestry, and related business activities. They may serve an area from ten to thirty miles in radius, and more than likely they have a large store from a national retail chain while older, indigenous businesses are seeking to find a niche market in which to survive. Typically, Agravilles have their own schools, some medical facilities, and government services. They are likely to have several churches, and often one fairly large church with significant influence in local affairs—the home church of a number of community leaders. Agravilles tend still to have a Main Street or a courthouse square.

"Mighthavebeenvilles" are described by Sim as towns that have lost much of their independence and self-sufficiency as they have had to yield local control to nearby Agravilles. Schools may have been lost to consolidation. Main Street often features several boarded-up stores, as people do little shopping locally, preferring the prices and variety to be found in Agravilles. Social services must also be obtained in Agraville. Some churches may have closed, and supporting a pastor financially is a major issue for the congregations that remain. Mighthavebeenvilles exist in relation to Agravilles in a manner somewhat analogous to the way Ribbonvilles relate to an urban area.

Finally, in Sim's typology, "Fairviews" are small towns that have created a new identity apart from whatever first shaped them. Recreational centers, retirement communities, and artist colonies can all be Fairviews. Such small towns might also be focused on a college, a military base, or even a prison. They are sometimes Mighthavebeenvilles that found a way to survive and even thrive. The local economy is often based on providing services for seasonal visitors. Considerable new construction may be evident. Fairview churches are challenged to provide ministry both for residents and visitors (the two groups probably have very different expectations); they may find attendance highest at unusual times of year because of an influx of vacationers or other visitors.

These four categories of small towns are not absolute; a given small town may exhibit characteristics of more than one type. A Ribbonville may still have a grain elevator to service farms lying beyond it, away from the city. A Mighthavebeenville may have a medical clinic providing health services locally. An Agraville may have some of the characteristics of a Ribbonville if good highways provide ready access for commuters to a nearby city. A Fairview may also serve as the center of a regional economy if a national retailer has moved in. But considering which of these four types best characterizes a town will be helpful. It is a starting point for understanding the specific context. Whatever their type, small towns are rarely sleepy little hamlets where nothing changes or happens. Rather they are confronted with an array of challenges according to their type. They may be growing or declining in population and commercial activity; often they face significant questions of identity. Will what has gone before cohere in some way with what is coming, or will the changes overwhelm the small town's previous identity?

Geographical Context

Whatever its type, each small town is located in a specific geographical context, and that geography shapes the residents. Many people may have been part of the local environment for so long that they no longer readily distinguish its influence on themselves. Sheer familiarity makes it hard to see. The minister, as a newcomer, not only needs to understand that geography; she may also be able to bring its power and importance into the consciousness of the congregation in ways that celebrate and confirm identity.

The small-community minister needs to get in the car and drive around the land that is the small town's environment. It is wise to take along someone who can help reveal the nuances and significance of what is seen. Learning the landscape and how it shapes the town's sense of reality is an important initial step in small-town ministry. Is the land so flat that neighbors can see one another's homes across surprising distances, or so carved up into hollows that folk struggle with isolation? Do the mountains or sky or sea dwarf human settlement? Are there forests or grassland or desert? What kind of wildlife is present? Does some natural feature function as a symbol of the area? What kinds of trees and crops grow? Is the land so steep that it is good only for pasture, or terraced to allow farming? Has a river defined the town's borders, and have its floods determined where people live? Are there levees or logging roads or lakeshores? Has the landscape been damaged by extractive activity (such as coal mining) or commercial development?

Here is a small portion of Drake Hokanson's description of the landscape around his small home town of Peterson, Iowa:

> Peterson . . . is a rural place, an agricultural place. Conversations in the bank, on the street, at a church smorgasbord may not always start on agricultural topics, but they are never far from the affairs of land, weather, machinery, markets. The town hides along the river in a valley filled with trees, a protected place of woods and echoes and diminished winds. Many people will tell you that Peterson is safe from tornados, that a tornado can't dip down into such a pronounced valley. But up on the flatlands, where a tornado can take a long aim at your house, the trees shrink back to hold only farmsteads and occasional ravines. Here farm groves stand as islands in an ocean of square fields, and the wind can blow to make souls lose their sanity.
>
> Row crops, trees and grasses cover every bit of soil around here: corn and soybeans where it is flat and square, trees throughout the valley, and grass everywhere else, filling in between all things. In miles of road ditches, in sidewalk cracks in town, holding sandbars in the river, in a pot of geraniums indoors, grasses are the predominant texture of this place. Native and imported grasses surround every field, follow every road, suffuse every neglected corner. By growing in the interstices and along the edges they make a mesh, a matrix; grasses provide the network which holds everything else in place.[4]

How does the weather shape life? Is this towering thundercloud country or coastal hurricane territory? When does the rain or the snow come, and how much? How do people cope with it? How hot, how cold does it get? Does some winter storm or summer drought linger in local legend? What's the wind like, and what fragrances does it carry—the grape aroma of a vineyard, the dust of a coal mine, the dry scent of wheat, the odor of a paper mill? Does it rustle through cornfields or cotton fields or trees? Can you hear traffic on a distant interstate, the lapping of waves, birds at daybreak, crickets at night? Is this a place where stars can be seen even in town? How does the setting of this small town "feel"?

All these sensory details are deeply part of small-town people for the simple reason that small towns live in a closer and more dynamic relation to the landscape than do urban and suburban places. Understanding and appreciating the power of landscape is crucial to understanding the people shaped by it. Besides the observational travels suggested above, listening to people talk will again and again reveal the significance of the landscape in their lives. Farmers, of course, talk about the weather, but other folk will speak of a bend in the river that is perfect for a picnic, or a trail where the wildflowers are better than anywhere else, or a patch of woods that never fails to produce a turkey in hunting season. What was lost when the mine was expanded or the forest logged or the river dammed? People may become concerned, even angry, if the landscape is abused by pollution or new development; or, on the other hand, acquiesce in despair if there seems no alternative for economic survival. Their sense of self may feel violated when the land of which they are a part is ravaged.

In Fairviews, Mighthavebeenvilles, Agravilles, and Ribbonvilles, landscape exploration will begin to unfold key elements of the local economy. The presence and impact of agriculture, extractive activity, or recreational development will become clear, as will the relationship with the services the town provides to those engaged in such economic activities. The grain elevator, the logging-truck service center, the ski-equipment shop make concrete the tie between land and town. The land shapes both inward personal reality and outward economic activity.

In addition to the geography of the surrounding country, attention should be given to the geography of the town itself. This learning is best done on foot, by walking through the community. Such a strolling tour will allow a rich, sensory image of the town to take shape.

> The small town image consists of sounds, smells, conversations, vistas, and emotions. It is a paradoxical truth that we slowly create our small towns in our image, and then they slowly rebuild us in theirs. Image is subtle, yet in determining what we value about small towns, it possesses great power.[5]

In walking the small town where I live, I learned quickly that the people of the African-American community came from Chicago, first as summer vacationers and later as permanent residents; that there had once been a minor-league baseball team, complete with a stadium that was a focal point of community recreation; that the first hospital had been located in the town physician's majestic home called "Bonnie Castle"; and that a Carnegie library had evolved into a small art musuem.[6]

If interruptions by rivers or coastlines are few, streets are often laid out on a regular north-south, east-west grid pattern that bespeaks order. If situated on a river or coast, small-town streets may take the water as the basis of their parallel and perpendicular runs, emphasizing the crucial character of the water, at least when the town was begun. Very old communities may have wandering lanes defined by almost forgotten destinations.

Many small towns do indeed have a Main Street (or State Street or High Street or Front Street or Broadway) or a town square at their heart. And this heart of the town is worth careful study.

> At the crossroads of commerce and transportation, civic identity and spatial range, Main Street provided both a convenient entrepôt and a material definition of citizenship for countless communities across the land. It was public space structured by common activity or need and gave to the people's experience a rich body of limits and metaphors.[7]

When is there traffic on Main Street, and when not? When are the "sidewalks rolled up"? Is there a train depot, and what is it used for now? Historical society or restaurant, perhaps? What is the mix of stores, and what businesses have closed? Are there goods and services that must be sought in other communities? Have consignment shops and antique stores replaced local retailers? Look up at the second stories of buildings—sometimes façades meant to impress in an earlier day—and note the dates when they were erected. Of what materials are the buildings constructed?

> [T]he chronology of Main Street is easily read in the materials used to build its structures. A glance at either side of the street reveals a variety of media: wood, brick, a small bit of high-quality dimension stone, and an occasional foundation laid up with round glacial rocks, stone boated in from hills and fields. There are walls of sheet and block glass, cinder block, concrete, aluminum, and even plastic. There is [a] clear time line here, one expressed in a

sequence of structural building materials starting with wood, moving to brick, then to what must be called assorted materials, and finally, to metal.[8]

Almost certainly, there will be at least one restaurant or café in which shifts of regulars take their turns at breakfast, coffee, and lunch—a place where

> [t]he coffeepot stands within easy reach of customers, and the morning [paper], already well shuffled, waits in an untidy pile nearby. The décor is basic café premodern, with paneled walls and Formica tabletops with some sort of pattern that looks like amoebas or boomerangs. [There is] a table reserved for nonsmokers, but no one pays attention.[9]

But are there other places where people can gather—recreation centers, for example? If mail is not delivered in town, as is often the case in quite small towns, the post office will be an important gathering and communication center. All these places should be visited and lingered in. Eat in the restaurants, wander in the stores, roll a few games at the bowling alley. Pick up several editions of the local newspaper and give them close attention. And if there is a local radio station, listen to it, because it is a sure bet the locals do.

Away from Main Street, spend time looking at neighborhoods. Are there any parks, and who or what is memorialized by any monuments? Is there an "other side of the tracks" area (perhaps quite literally), an affluent section, or is the town rather uniform in housing type? Where are the churches located vis-à-vis Main Street and neighborhoods? What denominations are represented? Where are the schools and government buildings, if any? Where does the town end and the surrounding country begin? And at the edge of town, do you find fast-food franchises, a strip mall, and a large retail store that are forcing Main Street to reinvent itself?

The internal geography of the small town shapes strongly the rhythms and patterns of life. "[T]he pace of small town life [is] played out on an intensely human scale, in terms comprehensible to most [people.]"[10] If people can walk to some of the places they need to visit in a course of errands, more time is available for the conversation that is so important as a means of small-town communication. If stores close early, people working out of town may find it hard to shop at local businesses, and thus may be partially cut off from the communication flow. So many little facets of life shape what happens in small communities, and time must be taken to sense their power and influence.

Finally, people who have lived in a small town for years will often describe the geography, both natural and constructed, in terms of what used to be. An auto-parts store may be described as "the old five-and-dime" or directions given to "make a right turn where the Randolph farm was, before the landfill got put in." It is not at all uncommon for a home to be described by naming the various families who lived in it over the years, often going back several generations. Listening for how the geography has changed will not only identify the longest-term residents, but will also offer openings into the history of the community.

It has been said, "[K]nowing who you are is impossible without knowing where you are."[11] The small-town minister who takes the time needed to learn the landscape will come to know his people more quickly and deeply.

CHAPTER 2

History

A small town is, of course, more than the result of its natural and engineered geography; it is the product of what has come to pass over time. Understanding the small town's history is essential for a number of reasons. As its residents meet the present and confront the future, they do so out of an indwelling sense of the past, a living story that is widely shared and cherished. History is alive, active, and oral in ways not often found outside small towns. The town's longest-term residents will usually know this history best, but all those who have come to belong to the community will know its essential outlines and its most famous, and infamous, incidents. And newcomers may begin to be accepted as they evidence some understanding of local history.

The town's present reality has evolved from how and why it began, from the challenges it has met, from the traditions that have grown over time, and from the sharing of all of this history from generation to generation. The lower mobility of small-town residents allows them to live into the history of the place even as they share in writing new chapters. In short, the past, though certainly not the only or even the most powerful influence (e.g., demographic and economic factors are others), shapes the present in small towns by shaping those now living. To take one dark example, it should not surprise us that the militia/hate-group movement (born in part, it has been suggested, of the farm crisis of the 1980s[1]) arose largely in parts of the country historically understood as the frontier, where taking the law into one's own hands was not uncommon. Just as geography decisively shapes life in small towns, so does historical experience.

The Problem of Preconceived Image

An almost universally experienced barrier to discovering the history of a small town is the internal image of small-town America that a minister brings to the context. This image, no matter where it falls on the spectrum from small town as romantic ideal to small town as narrow and backward, can blind one to the true story of a small community. Such images are born of the persistent fascination with small towns in American life—in literature[2] and, more recently, in media such as radio, television, and films (see bibliography). Two problems with these image-creating media: They tend toward a bipolar representation of towns as either wonderful or terrible, and they ignore the uniqueness of each small town. The popularity of Garrison Keillor's Lake Wobegon stories bespeaks our culture's ongoing interest in small towns. The value of his presentation of small-town life resides partly in its usually balanced image of a small town as a place with both good points and bad, virtues and vices, triumphs and failures.

> He tells us of all the little everyday problems of living together in a small community, frankly acknowledges intolerance, pettiness and boredom, as well as the comfortable spirit of community and togetherness.[3]

Particularly in the last chapter of his book *Lake Wobegon Days*, Keillor makes sure the reader understands that small-time life is not all peaches and cream by including "95 Theses" recording the damage perceived by a young person who grew up in Lake Wobegon.[4] Small towns are "both/and" places rather than "either/or." They can be nurturing and supportive as well as smothering and censorious.

To get past the limitations of one's internal image of small communities, I strongly recommend reading more sociologically based material early on in one's exploration. (See bibliography for publication information.) Excellent resources include *Worlds Apart*, by Cynthia M. Duncan (who examines small towns in northern Maine, Appalachian Kentucky, and the Mississippi Delta); *Main Street Blues*, by Richard O. Davies (Ohio); *Against All Odds*, by John C. Allen and Don A. Dillman (Washington); *Community and the Politics of Place*, by Daniel Kemmis (Montana); *Home Town*, by Tracy Kidder (Massachusetts); *Praying for Sheetrock*, by Melissa Fay Greene (Georgia); *Reflecting a Prairie Town*, by Drake Hokanson (Iowa);

and *Blue Highways* (all across America), by William Least Heat-Moon. All these books provide profoundly insightful glimpses into particular towns, and will give the small-town minister a truer vision of what is actually to be found there. Helpful novels include T. R. Pearson's *A Short History of a Small Place*, set in North Carolina; Jane Smiley's *A Thousand Acres*, set in Iowa; and Kent Haruf's *Plainsong*, set in Colorado. A unique and particularly valuable nonfiction book is Kathleen Norris's *Dakota*, which combines keen insight into small-town life with theological reflection.

For those wishing to learn and use a deep and systematic approach to understanding a small-town context in its richness, the materials from the Rural Social Science by Extension Program of the Agricultural Extension Service of Texas A&M University, edited by Gary Farley and Gary Goreham, and the writings of Shannon Jung (see bibliography) are excellent. The material on context for ministry in *Handbook for Congregational Studies*, edited by Jackson Carroll, Carl Dudley, and William McKinney, is also worthwhile as it offers analytical tools for systematic contextual study.

A minister coming to a small town might reasonably turn to any available written histories for insight into the past. These resources, available at libraries and historical societies, can be useful, particularly in describing the broad outlines of what has transpired there over time. In these can be found information on matters of importance such as the town's origin. What brought this small town into being? Did it spring up along a railroad line, as today's suburbs sprout along interstate highways radiating from cities? Was it first a port, a mill site, a fort, a mining camp? Who were its first residents, and what were their origins?

However, such written histories often do not tell the whole story (or the story as it is presently recalled), and they are prone to "boosterism."[5] A bias toward the past can create other problems with written local histories.

> One popular form of writing on the Plains is the local history. These books reveal a great deal about the people who write them but do not often tell the true story of the region. In North Dakota, most homesteaders failed to remain on their land after proving up a claim, and the 1920s and 1930s brought farm bankruptcies and political upheaval, but you would never know it to read local histories, centered on those who made it. They present tales of perseverance made heroic in the context of the steady march of progress from homesteading days to the present. As one old-timer told me,

"people have been writing it the way they wished it had been
instead of the way it was." The local history mentality that takes
care not to offend the descendants of pioneer families who had
grit enough to remain must . . . present the past "as a harmonious
whole" that, despite its hardships, was preferable to the present.[6]

It has also been noted that

the most profound impact of local history upon newcomers is not
made by refurbished historical buildings, or ethnic pageants, or
even the publications or exhibits of the historical society. No, the
history . . . is deeply ingrained into individual attitudes, social habits, environmental orientations . . . and many other vague and
elusive aspects of "life styles."[7]

History-Gathering

With these cautions in mind as to which written word to trust, and about
which to be cautious, history-gathering can begin in earnest. And as befits
biblical people grounded in narrative and oral tradition, much of this history-
gathering can best be done by listening to stories and asking the right questions. Indeed, one of the best features of small towns is the rich, oral library
of stories, and folk well able to tell them. The stories they tell are not just
stories, but "who we are."[8] And in listening well, the small-town minister
will be strengthened to resist the temptation to import programs and techniques that worked wonderfully well elsewhere, in a suburb or city, or even
another small town. Listening validates the speaker and his or her experience, and shows the minister to be one who respects where people are and
starts there.

A good place to begin is place names. If there are places (rivers, mountains, communities, etc.) with names of Native American origin, what do
they mean, and who were the first people here? Are there roads or cross-
roads named after families? Who were they, where did they come from,
how many generations lived along those roads, and are any of those families still in the area? How did the town get its name? Why did people
come here? To find a better life or to escape a situation somewhere else,
perhaps? Have there been later waves of immigration or an exodus of

residents? Where from and where to? Was there a glory period or a time of dark days? A defining flood or fire or tornado or hurricane or avalanche? What used to be here that is now missed? A movie theater or drive-in? A general store, hardware store, or bakery? Who were the memorable community members—a beloved town doctor who delivered many of the town's babies, a world traveler who returned, a politician who moved on to state or national office, a decorated war hero, a legendary teacher whose class everyone had to pass to graduate? Who is buried in the cemetery? Are there many stones with the same name or some large, imposing markers? What makes this town different from other nearby towns? What has been the greatest challenge the town has faced in the last ten years?

Often such questions will eventually evoke a response such as, "You'll have to ask old Mrs. So-and-So about that." Almost every small town has one, or perhaps a few, elders who are living links to even the fairly distant past. And it is worth seeking them out. Not so long ago, I buried a 91-year-old man who, as a boy, had stoked the church furnace and listened to stories told by folk who were old-timers then. As it turned out, they were among the founders of the church, begun in 1846. And he was a living link to a time usually accessible only in old books and photographs. A similar story:

Bat Nelson [the town barber] has been alive in every decade of this century and we began to talk about all the changes he had seen in his life since he was born on September 3, 1900. He paused and went over to one of the cabinets where he opened a drawer and took out a dog-eared notebook. It was a sort of "Doomsday Book" where on each page he had dutifully written the names of all of his friends, which from the number of entries I judged to have been all the residents of Alta Vista during the last half-century. Beside every name he had recorded the day each had died. As he read their names aloud I imagined he could see them coming through the door, and that for the moment he had brought them back to life again. He paused here and there to reminisce about someone or another, always having something kind to say about them. . . . When he came to the last page he closed the covers slowly, put the book away again in the drawer, and began to describe Alta Vista as it was sixty years ago. His memory was remarkable, and I listened raptly as he proceeded to run through the litany of place that had once been the heart and soul of a thriving town.[9]

It should be noted, of course, that such living historians may or may not be part of the congregation the small-town minister is to serve. If not, they can often give an unusually rich view of that congregation's historic role in the community, and how that role has changed through time. It will prove most helpful to ask a wide variety of people who are not members of the congregation what they think about that church—a police officer, a school-board member, the funeral director, the football coach, an elementary-school student, a small-business owner.[10] And community role is a good question to explore with folk within the church as well.

It is important to listen not just to the elderly historians of the town, but to hear how succeeding generations see the town as well. This work of listening should include youth and children, particularly to sense how the town's history is being conveyed from one generation to the next. Furthermore, take note of the local language in which the history is told. Inflection, repeated anecdotes, local idioms, and grammatical constructions all help construct the local ethos. What Kathleen Norris says of language on the Plains is true in other places:

> On the Plains, I have . . . drunk in the language of unschooled people, a language I was not exposed to within the confines of the academic and literary worlds. Many farmers I know use language in a way that is as eloquent as it is grammatically unorthodox. Their speech often has great style; they never use a wrong word or make an error in phrasing. . . . Language here still clings to its local shading and is not yet corrupted by the bland usage of mass media. We also treasure our world-champion slow talkers, people who speak as if God has given them only so many words to use in a lifetime, and having said them they will die.[11]

If, in the course of this history-gathering, a particular event emerges as crucial to the town's identity—a natural disaster, a new industry locating there, the beginning or ending of rail service—it will probably be worth the time to dig out copies of newspapers from the time of the event. Church records may also shed some light on it. A factual perspective balanced with how the event is told in the town's oral tradition will afford a helpful understanding of both the event itself and how it functions in local lore. Both what happened and how it is remembered shape the community's self-understanding.

It is more difficult to gain an understanding of the underside of a small town—perhaps because of a boosterism that does not want to talk much about elements that do not conform to the town's self-image. But most small towns have an underside of people who are at the margins, perhaps because of work schedules, income level, race or ethnicity, addiction, or mental illness. Having a cup of coffee at one o'clock in the morning with the clerk of an all-night convenience store or sitting in a tavern after a shift change at a local factory will open a different perspective on the town, as will riding with a law-enforcement officer on an evening shift or walking with a letter carrier through the town's neighborhoods. The answers to the questions cited earlier may be quite different when they come from people at the margins, and their responses help complete the image of the town.

History-taking in the small town is a task never completed. As long as a minister serves in a small community, it will prove valuable to listen to people of every age and circumstance tell about the town. The more history the minister learns, the more he or she will understand the traditions and beliefs that shape the town's encounter with the present. And such knowledge will ground the local congregation's history and tradition in their larger context.

In some denominations,

> [r]eligious leaders at the local level are moved from one community to another every three to five years. In a community with [a very strong] tie to the past, three to five years is not long enough to develop relationships with the locals. The community-control norms are often unseen by the new religious leaders.[12]

Intentional history-taking is key to reducing the time needed to get to know the locals and their community, and thereby to offer in an acceptable manner the gifts the minister brings—gifts that may be helpful not only to the congregation, but to the community as a whole.

CHAPTER 3

Culture

S mall communities are complex yet usually comprehensible places. Each small town has its own way of constellating itself, and yet there are common themes in the way small towns generally approach such matters as economics, politics, social life, education, communication, and the annual cycle of events. A good measure of understanding these dimensions of small-town life is essential to the minister, particularly before he or she seeks to intervene or encourage change. Small towns are confronted with changes in each of the areas named above. Economics are changing rapidly with the advent of globalization, the horizontal and vertical integration of farming and other economic sectors (e.g., the buyout of local pharmacies by regional chains),[1] the Information Age, and the arrival of new commercial enterprises. Politics are often becoming more open as people assert their rights, as women assume political offices, and as newcomers replace established leadership. Social life, as lived out in diverse small groups, may be strained in its ability to provide relief from the increased stress brought on by change. Education is central to many aspects of small-town life—identity through time, transmission of history and norms to succeeding generations, employment, and sometimes conflict. Powerful, effective, and often informal communication networks help hold small communities together and are a key part of decision-making processes. Small-town life is shaped by a cycle of events that structure time and reinforce traditions. Understanding all these aspects of small-town life is important, particularly as the minister seeks to respond to the needs and challenges confronted by the community and church.

Economics

Time was, and not so long ago, when many a small town was the center of a small local economy. Supporting a small area with needed retail outlets and services, and serving as a connection to the larger world, were what made small towns run. Often towns were remarkably self-contained. That situation probably began unraveling with the arrival of the Sears & Roebuck catalog, which meant that almost anything could be shipped almost anywhere the trains ran, and that was almost everywhere.[2]

The discovery of small towns by corporate America and national retailers, as well as the dawn of the Information Age, has dramatically accelerated the pace of economic change.[3] It is not uncommon, for example, to find fast-food franchises even in Mighthavebeenvilles. The arrival of a Wal-Mart, or other large national or regional retailer, can solidify a Mighthavebeenville's conversion into an Agraville, even as it threatens local businesses with extinction. In certain agricultural regions, such as the area from North Dakota to Texas, the farm crisis of the 1980s and the continuing consolidation and vertical integration of farming have been major factors reshaping the economies of small towns.

> The same economy of scale that makes it impossible for the dime store or the local drugstore to compete with Wal-Mart increasingly gathers farm ground into ever bigger and bigger parcels.[4]

Fewer farms mean fewer people, and potentially the end of a Mighthavebeenville's existence. Furthermore, people migrating to small towns seeking a better quality of life are "bringing their money with them."[5] This, too, impacts the small town economically, usually positively. Retirees moving to a small town will usually bring new financial resources to be spent in that town, while new residents who commute may draw on local services but do a significant portion of their spending in their work community. The conversion of a Mighthavebeenville into a Fairview may benefit many who can integrate into a resort- or retirement-based economy, but not everyone will be able to make such a transition.

Such changes can leave small-town people living in more than one world simultaneously. While wanting to continue old patterns and traditions, they may also have availed themselves of the manifold advantages of technology.

A farmer would think nothing of buying and selling future[s] con-
tracts by telephone [or computer] through a commodities broker,
yet the same farmer would not consider using no-till production
methods because of the "kidding he would have to take" from
other farmers. Another farmer would visit several out-of-town
automobile dealers trying to get the "best deal" on a new car, but
simply call up the local fertilizer dealer and ask for thousands of
dollars worth of fertilizer to be delivered, without asking the price.[6]

The arrival of a new industry in a small town can also be a mixed
reality. On the one hand, it offers the prospect of "good jobs" (with benefits,
as opposed to the "bad jobs" without benefits[7]) but may also drive up land
values, forcing people off farms, out of homes, even out of the community.[8]
Similarly, the opening of a Wal-Mart, while causing some stores to close,
may stimulate others to become more competitive;[9] and while making a
Mighthavebeenville into an Agraville (with a better chance for survival),
deals harsh economic blows to other nearby Mighthavebeenvilles. Securing
one small town on the map may ensure that another small town will eventually and permanently disappear from that map.

So while economic development of various kinds may ensure the survival or enhance the economic viability of a small town, it does not come
without costs. These costs may be felt in surrounding communities, and
most certainly will shake the fabric of the close-knit small town. Most of
these changes mean that in one way or another, poverty is a significant
reality for numerous small-town people. Mighthavebeenvilles can shrivel up
into "rural ghettos."[10] In many regions the rate of rural poverty is higher
than that of urban areas.[11] It does not take much looking to find a good
number of families living in trailers on a relative's land or doubling up in
homes.

A particularly harsh situation can arise when a small town is economically dependent on a single factory or mine or small group of landowners.
Here the class division between haves and have-nots can be dramatic, with
the elite controlling employment, political life, and education. This situation
may be more common in some parts of the country than others; it is one that
a minister serving in a small town certainly should be aware of. It warrants
special study and understanding.[12]

Furthermore, economically threatened small towns may be vulnerable
to jumping at any economic opportunity that comes along. The chance to

survive by becoming some kind of Fairview is enticing. But such an economic change may bring new problems along with the possibility of survival.

> Given the economic depression of much of rural America, the temptation to accept new functions for old towns will be great. . . . [T]wo of the major growth industries are prisons and dumps. In a sense, urban America is looking to rural America as a place to get rid of its refuse—material and human. . . . Further, be careful of the developers of new retirement towns and recreational facilities. Some have spoiled the natural beauty . . . [and] have shoved aside and exploited the long-time residents.[13]

People are stressed by economic change, even if such changes stabilize or even improve small-town life. Because of the strong relational ties in a small town, the community suffers when some members are hurt by change and may have to leave the community while others prosper. Likewise, the influx of newcomers due to economic changes is stressful. The Internet, satellite uplinks, and cable television bring the world much closer—and also bring influences both positive and negative. New business may be enabled to locate in small towns by such technology. But at the same time, the arrival of these technologies can make small-town life increasingly private at the expense of the sense of community previously cherished.

Small towns are feeling the impact of numerous and often large economic changes. Some are good, some bad. Some are life-enhancing, some nearly fatal to the town's previously known character. Sensing the changes and their impact on individual members and all social classes of the community is an important work of justice for the small-town minister. The question of who benefits and who is hurt by economic change should be kept in mind, and constantly held up before the small community.

Politics

> Of course, in politics some things never change. A few years back the mayor got into a battle with the DPW and tried to force the chairman of its board to resign. The mayor often talked about openness in government, but when the chairman refused, she went behind the scenes and threatened privately not to reappoint one of

his friends. The DPW got even. It snowed a fair amount that winter, and the mayor and her neighbors often found their street unplowed. About half of the present council, and the mayor herself, had come to Northampton as adults, as sophisticated people, bringing new ideas to town, ideas formed out in the wider world. But they brought them to a stage that hadn't really changed. It was still very small.[14]

Having lived around the corner from a small-town mayor who was on good terms with the Department of Public Works, I enjoyed marvelously clean streets one very snowy winter. Political life works this way in small towns. And although the stage may be small, it is changing, as evidenced by the movement of women and newcomers into political office in small towns. Often, it is their time, energy, expertise, and new ideas that are needed. And yet, old patterns and personalities may continue to shape political life. This may be especially true in communities dominated by one industry whose leadership composes a de facto ruling elite. These people may not hold public office in the community but have significant influence over who does.[15] Politics in such places is often not the more open process of an economically diverse town. In every small-town context it is important to discern if segments of the community are being excluded from the political process (often by being shut out of informal communication systems) for reasons of economic class, race, or ethnicity.

Often in small towns, one of two patterns has prevailed. The same folk may have held positions of influence (town council, school board, township supervisor) for long periods, or there is a pattern of succession, with established members of the community expected to take their turn in providing service and leadership. Municipal government may or may not be the most influential political body in small-town life. It is not uncommon, for example, for the school board to be more important, particularly if the schools are one of the larger employers in the area.[16]

Furthermore, the mix of formal and informal positions of influence makes political life complex. Often what happens in coffee shops and other gathering places outside formal meetings is more significant than the meetings themselves. For example, the story of a small town in Washington state told in *Against All Odds* includes a compelling example of a school-board meeting in which consolidation with another district was under consideration. Public comment was intense, often emotional, and unanimously opposed to the action. And yet, just one week later, the board voted for the consolidation without a voice raised publicly in protest.

> To an outside observer, the contrast between the trauma of the first meeting and the quiet acquiescence of the second may seem at best impossible. At worst, it might be seen as a sign of protest without commitment, psychological withdrawal, and powerlessness. Nothing could be further from reality.[17]

This astonishing turn of events was made possible by hours and hours of conversation by the board members at coffee shops explaining why controlled consolidation was the community's best option in light of state mandates, enrollment patterns, and staffing alternatives. This is a good example of the complexity of small-town politics and how it often works.

In that same small town, however,

> No woman had served on the . . . school board until 1979. Since that time some members of the community have perceived the movement of women and a few new residents onto the board as a sign that the power of the school board should be decreased.[18]

Again, the complex mix of the old and new is clear. A change in the pattern of who leads makes some small-town people anxious, raising questions not only about the place of women and newcomers in the political order, but about the order itself. There is a pull, of varying strength, toward holding onto what, and who, has worked in the past. This tendency can create friction and stress.

In small communities, political labels such as party affiliation or "liberal" and "conservative" are rarely used. Where people tend to know one another, or to be able to learn quickly about others, such labels have little meaning. Furthermore, historically a great deal of special training has not been needed for specific local offices, so individuals often serve at various times in several different offices.[19] This situation can tend toward control by a few people, but it is not often abused. The value of reputation is usually high enough to temper the temptation to misuse power.

All that said, the challenges confronting small towns, from the possibility of extinction to economic development to demographic changes to urban encroachment, often mean that old approaches to political matters are not adequate. Sometimes newcomers are exactly what is needed—people with expertise and experience in grant-writing, in dealing with larger political entities such as state and national agencies, and so forth. Old leaders may simply get discouraged fighting to preserve their town, and out of fatigue be willing to release their grip on the reins of power.[20]

Comprehending the small-town political system takes time, and understood it must be if the minister and her congregation anticipate taking part in dealing with impending changes. The combining of old and trusted patterns and people with the new approaches needed to engage contemporary problems is a complex process. Inappropriate or naïve involvement in the political realm can damage a minister's credibility substantially and quickly. Taking the time to listen, to watch, to get to know the players and the processes will be time well spent.

Social Life

> The American Legion does Memorial Day and funds the expenses of the town baseball team. The Lions [C]lub has a barbecue and fireworks display to celebrate the Fourth of July. The volunteer fire department handles the Old Settlers Days. Community celebrations of Easter Sunrise and [T]hanksgiving are organized by the Ministerial Alliance. The Garden Club beautifies the city park.[21]

Social groups, both formal and informal, are critical to small-town life. In communities not dominated by a single industry or too small to have much in the way of government services, they are often what keeps community life going.[22] In addition to groups such as those noted above, Masonic lodges, the Grange, women's clubs, sports associations (e.g., bowling leagues), retiree groups, and the Chamber of Commerce may all have a part in shaping the town socially. It is sometimes surprising just how many such groups may be found in a small community, but the sense that there is much to be done to keep life going and that everyone needs to play a constructive part contributes to the number of functioning social groups. Churches are an important part of the pattern of social groups, particularly as they offer activities open to the whole town. And often churches will specialize and take care not to compete with each other in such activities. The Baptists won't have their annual out-of-town revivalist come at the same time the Methodists are holding their annual craft fair.

Such groups serve a number of functions in small communities. They not only are responsible for maintaining activities that are part of the community's traditional ritual life; they may also spearhead or support new programs to enhance community vitality, such as downtown redevelopment projects, support of school improvements, or perhaps the building of a community swimming pool. These groups are also crucial to the flow of information. Issues discussed in meetings may help build consensus before a matter comes to public or official consideration.[23]

Informal groups, like the succession of coffee klatches that come through a local café every weekday morning, are also key parts of the town's communication system. This "Café Society" often endures through many years, is as regular as clockwork, and is indispensable to keeping the fabric of the small town intact.

> [C]onversation is often served as a main dish with coffee on the side. Most customers are well acquainted with one another but don't necessarily socialize outside their encounters . . . at the café. Many interactions are intended merely to pass the time of day, an enduring small town tradition; some share gossip. Others, though it might be hard to tell with only a casually tuned ear, exchange real information and reinforce bonds of friendship and respect.
>
> [C]afés have certain daily, seasonal, and climatic rhythms. Sue's is a morning place, and each weekday she has two morning crowds. The first is the steady and punctual bunch that comes in right when the place opens—sometimes they are waiting at the door when she . . . unlocks it. [S]he feeds them and pours gallons of coffee. "The early risers like their sausage sandwiches," says Sue. "Later we have the women invade." Farm women, town women, retired women, they come in for their midmorning coffee before some people are even out of bed.[24]

In my town, four different cafés serve between two and four such groups each; and what one person in a group knows, they all know. The groups' longevity and intimate relationships are part of what strengthens the town to cope with impinging changes.

All of these groups serve another purpose—the relief of stress. While some people may seek out small-town life believing it to be less stressful, small-town life has its own tensions. These may not be the pressures of fast-paced urban life or the efforts needed to conform to suburban norms, but they can be quite significant. Not only do the economic changes create stress; so does the simple fact of being known, perhaps better than one might like to be. Small towns are not places to hide in anonymity.

While visiting in a small Arab town in Israel some years ago, I was startled to discover how quickly much became known about me. Within a day of my arrival, everyone knew who I was, where I was from, where I was staying, and for how long. "There's not much to do here," said my host, "so everyone is very aware of the smallest change." While American small towns may not be so quiet, the same habits of close observation and aware-ness of change are universal. This close attention is a two-edged sword. It can be nice to be known, to trust that someone has an eye on one's children, and that one's participation in and contribution to the community will be noted and valued. On the other hand, the sense that one's life is a public matter can be stressful indeed, particularly if one is coping with personal or relational problems. Discovering that the act of buying a new car will occa-sion a remarkable amount of public comment can be more than a little unnerving for people accustomed to a fair measure of anonymity and re-spect for privacy.

> Privacy takes on another meaning in such an environment, where you are asked to share your life, humbling yourself before the common wisdom, such as it is. Like everyone else, you become public property and come to accept things that city people would consider rude. A young woman using the pay phone in a West River café is scrutinized by several older women who finally ask her, "Who are you, anyway?" On discovering that she is from a ranch some sixty miles south, they question her until, learning her mother's maiden name, they are satisfied. They know her grand-parents; good ranchers, good people.[25]

Psychologically, it may well be that small communities are attractive in part as a solution to the problem of social isolation and feelings of personal insignificance experienced by many in mass culture, that they offer a social solution to a personal problem and an antidote to the negative aspects of individualism.[26] To the extent that this is so, participation in social groups is key to the individual as well as to the larger life of the community itself. In contrast to urban and suburban churches, where offering a sense of belonging may be essential to attracting and retaining new members, small-town churches may find that some of those needs are met through other groups in town, and the congregation may need to identify and address needs not being met elsewhere.

Education

Schools are always a key, if not *the* key, focal point of small-town life. In fact, the school district is often the defining geographical unit. Virtually all citizens living within the school district, which will often encompass a large region around the town proper, will think and speak of themselves as being from the town. If their children go to school there, it is their hometown.

Schools matter to small towns in many ways. They are significant centers of social life, not only for the children and youth who are involved in activities like sports, plays, club activities, and band, but also for parents, whose attendance at their children's activities and participation in supporting organizations like the Parent-Teacher Association and the sports boosters organization can take up much of their free time.

> Well, you can always tell when [our team] is playing. No one is in town or at home. If anyone every wanted to rob the whole town, that's the time to do it. It's about the only time . . . that someone isn't around to see if a strange car pulls up.[27]

School sports, particularly great teams or athletes from the past, are central to a small community's identity. Remembering the team that almost won the state championship and comparing it to the current team is more than a major topic of café conversation: It is how history lives in the present. Many a small town has a sign at the edge of town informing all who pass by that this is the home of the state-championship wrestling or baseball or football team in a certain year gone by.

> Sports have always been an integral part of small town life. Football in the fall, basketball in the winter, and baseball in the spring. The playing fields, gymnasiums, and field houses are very often the most prominent and newest facilities of most schools, which perhaps says something about academic priorities. It is true, too, there is hardly a town . . . that doesn't have a baseball diamond, be

it only a "sandlot" or playing field of some sort ringed all around with signs advertising the local merchants who sponsor the teams.[28]

But academics matter, too. While care may be taken not to emphasize former students who succeed in the larger world at the expense of those who continue to live in the small town (since they help provide a future for the town), pride is taken in the graduate who leaves town and achieves a measure of renown in academics or politics or business or entertainment. And those who go off to college are respected, particularly as they affirm the small town's value to them by making return visits. In small towns where poverty is a significant reality, schools are seen as a way out of a place where the future is limited. Of course, there is a sadness in the knowledge that a school's ensuring a future for the youth may damage the future of the town itself.[29]

Particularly in quite small towns, schools may be one of the larger employers in the area and play an important role in the local economy. They can be significant arenas for community conflict over such issues as personnel (particularly administrative but also faculty), facilities construction, and consolidation with other districts.[30]

Beyond all these matters, it is the school's role in inculcating a particular town's values to successive generations that secures its importance. School superintendents may see the small town as a stepping-stone to bigger positions, but teachers and staff tend to stay for long periods, even their whole careers. It is common to find faculty members who are products of the small-town school system in which they now teach, as well as teachers who grew up in other small towns where they learned to appreciate the gifts of small-town life. Teachers may have taught not only a student's older siblings, but even their parents.

This kind of continuity conveys both implicitly and explicitly the enduring quality of life in a given town, as does the annual cycle of school events—sports seasons, school plays and pageants, dances, graduations, trips. Residents of small towns often make tremendous efforts on behalf of schools, raising money for scholarships or for a team to travel to a special competition. Indeed, it has been suggested that the extremely strong expectation that local businesses will financially support such activities constitutes a "hidden tax" of doing business in a small town.[31] And damage can be done to the schools when large national retailers come to town, as they displace school-supportive local businesses but may themselves feel no obligation to support local programs.

Small-town schools may find themselves caught between conflicting goals. On the one hand, the community may highly value the school's role in teaching community pride and tradition and in having the students feel they are known and valued. On the other hand, residents are well aware of such forces as a rapidly changing economy in which many youth will make their lives elsewhere and need to be equipped to do so.[32] Helping students value their origins while preparing them for life elsewhere, and doing so in the face of limited resources and of mandates from state and federal authorities, is a daunting task.

Understanding local schools—their traditions, functioning, and personnel—and supporting them is important for the small-town minister, whether or not he or she has school-age children. Uninformed criticism or even lack of attendance at school events can seriously undermine the small-town minister's effectiveness. Supporting the schools with, for example, a service recognizing high-school graduates will markedly increase that effectiveness.

Annual Cycle of Events

A minister new to small-town ministry stubbornly went ahead and scheduled a meeting of the stewardship committee on the night before deer season opened, despite having been told that no one would attend. He was, of course, the only one who showed up, and drinking far too much of the pot of coffee he had made kept him up most of the night vowing not to make such a mistake again.

> People growing up in communities of memory not only hear the stories that tell how the community came to be, what its hopes and fears are, and how its ideals are exemplified in outstanding men and women; they also participate in the practices—ritual, aesthetic, ethical—that define the community as a way of life. We call these "practices of commitment" for they define the patterns of loyalty and obligation that keep the community alive.[33]

Time in small towns is given rhythm by the yearly cycle of events. These events not only affect the scheduling of church activities; they are occasions that deepen and convey community identity. Schools may close for a day during the county fair or for the opening of deer season. A town may pour itself into an annual water or mushroom or dogsledding or pioneer or old-car or music or harvest festival that draws everyone together to pull it off and inevitably invites telling stories of previous editions of the event. A bike race or car race or triathlon, a tour of historic homes, a rodeo, a sailing regatta, parades for school and civic occasions are other examples of such events. If the Lions Club has always cooked breakfast for the event, the club knows it has a valued place in town. Individuals holding certain positions in town will have specific functions they always perform (e.g., lead the parade, sell tickets, give an invocation), and a small-town minister may be one such person. Planning and executing such an event deepen the sense of belonging, mattering, and succeeding—all important parts of a small town's self-esteem. These events can often be important to the town economically if they draw large numbers of tourists. A town's well-done Fourth of July parade may turn out to be a big day for Main Street retailers.

Of particular note in this cycle of events is the autumn football homecoming game. A German student living with my family one year was utterly puzzled by all the commotion surrounding football homecoming. She simply could not grasp what the big deal was. And when I had first come to a small town, I had shared some of that puzzlement. What I have come to realize is that homecoming is more than an annual event—it is an important and multidimensional metaphor for small-town life. It is something of an antidote to the suspicion that small towns and their residents are somewhat outmoded in an urbanizing, suburbanizing, globalizing mass culture. When high-school alumni come back to town for an evening of parades, parties, and football, a sense is conveyed to the town that "We do matter. We helped make these kids into who they are. And we did a pretty good job."

But homecoming as a metaphor goes beyond football. From time to time, former residents will return to retire, and their return says there is something in the small town worth returning to. A good place to grow up in turns out to be a good place to grow old in as well. Not infrequently, former townspeople who have died elsewhere are brought "home" to be buried. This event occasions a lot of storytelling, reminiscing, and reacquaintance. And with these again comes a renewed sense of the town's making a difference. Sometimes a child of the community will, having explored the larger world, return home to live and work.[34]

[M]ost of the young people move on. But, as one couple recently told me of their daughter, "She's traveled, she's seen the outside world. And it's not that she's afraid of it or couldn't live there, she's decided she doesn't need it. She wants to come back here."[35]

In a world often rushing toward and anxious about the future, the metaphor of homecoming helps sustain small towns.

Just as the liturgical year is structured by times of preparation for a major festival (as Advent for Christmas, Lent for Easter), the times of celebration themselves, and times of reflection after the events, so these annual small-town events provide pattern and rhythm to life. They keep life moving, but not at such a rapid pace that there is no time for anticipation and savoring. The events of any small town will usually be spaced through the year so that they do not crowd in upon one another. They often show the town at its best, and offer a chance to see and hear and smell and taste and touch a lot of what makes the town what it is. Not only do town events need to be respected by the church calendar; they are essential aspects of the local culture.

Despite the pervasiveness of mass culture in the Information Age, small towns maintain some measure of distinctiveness in their cultures. This truth, along with the richness and complexity of those cultures, means that small-town ministers should take the needed time to discern carefully the cultural subtleties of the context in which they work.

CHAPTER 4

Values

S mall towns are distinguished by a number of distinctive values. Some, like cherishing community, may be obvious, while others to be discussed here—longevity in the community, sense of place, and forbearance—may not be. These values are part of what makes people feel safe in small towns—physically safe in the (now less common) not-locking-our-doors sense, and emotionally safe in the life-is-generally-predictable-here sense.

> The shopkeepers didn't cover their windows with steel grates after hours. Indeed, they left things outside that could easily have been defaced—flower boxes on the sidewalk, canvas awnings over the storefronts. Fragile things left out at night seemed to declare that the place was safe, and maybe they helped make it safer. Maybe people inclined to vandalism and assault usually behaved themselves here, not just because they realized there was a good chance of getting caught, but because they didn't want to mess up something they, too, enjoyed. . . . Visitors sensed, as people rarely do in a big city, that the place had a general code of correct behavior almost unanimously endorsed.[1]

What is striking about these values is that each of them has a paradoxical quality. There is for each one a counterpoint that is also definitive in shaping the contemporary small town.

Community

The sense of community is often what draws people to, and keeps people in, small towns. It can "provide meaning, a sense of belonging, and well-being" in addition to being a solution to the problems of isolation and ennui.[2] The sense of belonging in a small community is an alternative to excessive individualism and mass society.[3] The poet W. H. Auden lived in New York for over two decades, and yet late in life he returned to his native England, to the relatively small town of Oxford. He noted, "It's just that I am getting rather old to live alone in the winter and I'd rather live in community. Supposing I had a coronary. It might be days before I was found. At Oxford, I should be missed if I failed to turn up for meals."[4]

The feelings of being known, of having a role, of making contributions to public life that are noticed and valued, of participating in something worthwhile that is larger than the self, of being able to act compassionately on a personal level, of having journeyed through time with a group that generally accepts each member, warts and all—these feelings are strong and nourishing to small-town residents.

> In small towns every person had a place, no matter how insignificant. People knew each other by their first names, not by their telephone or fax numbers. They knew where each other lived, and who their fathers and mothers were. There was a network, stultifying at times to be sure, but always there if you were in need. A deal was often consummated by the shake of a hand, which was as good as a contract. Business was conducted slowly, perhaps over coffee in a cafe on Main Street, much in the manner of a baseball game which is not played by the clock; a reason perhaps why baseball has been called the national pastime.[5]

Of such is community made.

But in tension with community are several other values. One of these is personal freedom, a measure of which is often sacrificed for the sake of belonging.[6] Community can bestow its blessings only if most members act according to agreed-upon norms, are generally willing to go along with how things have been done before, and bow to majority consensus. Personal privacy is also in tension with the valuing of community. Gossip is a staple of small communities that is paid for with the currency of privacy.

> We are interrelated in a small town, whether or not we're related by blood. We know without thinking about it who owns that car; inhabitants . . . learn to recognize each other's footsteps in the hall. Story is a safety valve for people who live as intimately as that; and I would argue that gossip done well can be a holy thing. It can strengthen the communal bonds. Gossip provides comic relief for people under tension. . . . Gossip can help us give a name to ourselves. . . . Allowing yourself to be the subject of gossip is one of the sacrifices you make, living in a small town.[7]

The high valuing of community creates tension in the matter of what to do with newcomers. For the sake of reputation, small towns often present themselves, and are often perceived by visitors, as friendly places. And yet, new residents, not having shared the history and traditions, are sometimes viewed with suspicion, particularly if they are seen as importing urban or suburban values rather than desiring to take on rural ones. "The very characteristic [community] that makes the town desirable also makes it rejecting."[8] Welcoming newcomers, it is feared, will alter the precious feeling of community that has been slowly wrought over long years. And besides, it is work to keep teaching the history and traditions over and over instead of living them out with those who already know them well. Finally, many fear that welcoming newcomers to replace the dying old and the departing young will cost them their sense of belonging.

The sense of community that is born of a homogeneity of experience is sometimes companioned by a homogeneity of population—ethnically, racially, or religiously. Small towns are growing more diverse in these dimensions, and this too may create stress in the community. Social class is an issue as well in many small towns, and not all classes participate in the feeling of community the insiders enjoy. The outsiders

> might include persons who are there but do not want to participate (commuters, weekenders), the newcomers (for some reason not readily assimilable—race, culture, lifestyle, religion, vocation) and the underclass (exploited workers, temporary residents, the wounded).[9]

A friend from South Africa visiting my town noticed while traveling about that most of the physicians and several motel and restaurant owners were people of Asian origin. He noted, "This is just so much like South Africa! Certain ethnic groups have certain jobs deemed necessary. But are they part of the community?" Not in all ways, I had to answer.

People might also be excluded from the sense of community by affluence, particularly if they choose to keep to themselves by physically or psychologically "gating" themselves off. The unwritten rule seems long to have been that "as long as they avoided ostentation,"[10] and used their personal and financial resources to help strengthen the town, the affluent could be very much part of the community.[11]

The sense of community is certainly still to be found in small towns. Even those that are growing are still much shaped by the traditions, behaviors, and patterns crafted when the town was smaller. And yet, pulling at this distinguishing small-town value are other values and forces that cannot be avoided.

Longevity

As a corollary to the importance of history in small towns, longevity of presence is valued by residents. The longer one has lived in the town, the greater the likelihood that one has understood and accepted the town's norms and traditions. This valuing of long-term presence shapes the town in several ways. With regard to professionals who work in town, longevity often matters as much as, if not more than, skills and credentials. For example, local people will often keep going to the old, established physician, even as they complain about his or her shortcomings, instead of switching to a new physician with more up-to-date training.

> Small town people know that professionals, especially those who
> have or seek exceptional credentials, are likely to live among them
> for a short time before moving on to a place where they can earn
> more money and advance their careers.[12]

Unless there is a critical need for leadership, a minister new to a small community will need to stay for a number of years before being asked to serve on boards and committees that are influential in shaping the town's life. While I had always felt respected in town, it was not until I had hung around for six years (and didn't try to force my way in) that I began to be asked to serve on significant groups in the community. At a perhaps almost unconscious level, it had been decided I had been around long enough (and had earned my wings by understanding and valuing the community's identity) to be trusted with positions of some influence.[13]

But valuing longevity, while understandable and necessary in the pursuit of continuity, also can contribute to an acceptance of mediocrity.[14] Retaining what is good enough for the town just because it has been around a long time can crowd out what would be truly good for the town—new people, new ideas, new approaches to problems. Furthermore, leadership kept in the hands of a long-serving few tends either to burn them out or to consolidate control in too few people. Valuing longevity can protect the town from those who would seek to change it without understanding it, but doing so can also prevent the town from accepting new people who do understand it and could help it creatively meet new challenges.

Sense of Place

"Mobility and the profit motive blunt our sense of place, allowing the land to be bulldozed into a vast commercial way station."[15] That may well be so for much of the world, but it is not true in small towns. Place is highly valued, even more than time. The land surrounding the town is understood, and often cherished, in its supporting function. Small-town people sense their belonging not only to one another, but also to a specific locale.

> Many people had no better reason for living there than the place itself. For them it wasn't just anywhere, but the place they chose because they felt it had chosen them.[16]

The cycle of events mentioned earlier is grounded not only in the history of the place but in the place itself, and often celebrates and reconfirms what the place means. Even when the place is being subjected to extractive economic activities like mining and logging, attachment to it is strong. And in some areas, damage to the life-supporting ability of the local area may bring environmental concerns into better balance with economic necessity. Among religious people in small communities, this sense of place is often reflected in clearly articulated beliefs that "the earth is the Lord's" (Ps. 24:1) and that "the Lord is in this place" (Gen. 28:16).

But this attachment to place, this being defined by place, can lead some small-town residents toward provincialism and even fear of the larger world. And with the larger world pressing in ever more upon small towns—through technology, mass media, the discovery by corporate America—skills for coping with the larger world are essential if the very aspects of small-town life so cherished are to be preserved and sustained in some way.

> With such services [interlibrary loan] becoming commonplace, others might consider living in a remote area and commuting electronically to their workplaces. But the changes wrought by new information technology are not always welcome here. In one town, when the state library offered a public library access through a computer hook-up to millions of books in regional and national databases, the librarian did not want it. It seemed like an insult to her many years of dedicated service, suggesting that the decent but small collection she'd built was no longer good enough. Interlibrary loan is an unwelcome link to a larger world, forcing us to recognize that we're not as self-sufficient as we imagine ourselves to be. . . . Small towns need a degree of insularity to preserve themselves. But insularity becomes destructive when ministers, teachers, librarians grow weary of pretending not to know what they know, and either leave or cease to offer themselves as resources whose knowledge could benefit the community.[17]

A sense of place grounds people and keeps them from feeling adrift and directionless on the tides of mass culture and urban rootlessness. But it can also create blindness to the benefits to be gained from encounter with the larger world, and even induce a stonewalling mentality against that world.

Forbearance

A final value worth noting is that of forbearance. In living with a high degree of closeness, even intimacy, small-town people seem to know innately that they need to bear with one another. Realizing the damage that conflict can quickly do in close quarters, people tend to put up with one another and accept one another's foibles. They do not go to court at the drop of a hat. Within the confines of those norms essential to the maintenance of community life, considerable room remains for individual quirkiness. Having served in suburban contexts with their strange mix of isolation and conformity, I am struck by a small town's blend of belonging and accepting diversity. The odd, the different, the eccentric can find a home in a small town and even a role to play.

Not long after moving to town, I was waiting at one of the town's three traffic lights when a shabbily dressed older man, with heavily smudged glasses and a dirty stocking cap, knocked on the passenger window of my car with his cane. Without hesitating or waiting for me to respond, he got into the car and settled himself in the seat, carefully arranging bags full of newspapers and calendars. "Drive me out to Centreville," he said in a tone perfectly placed between a demand and a request. He didn't talk much as I drove, but he did say a few words about some points of interest along the way, telling me who had lived in a number of houses, and when. At last, he told me to stop in front of a certain house, thanked me, got out with his belongings and said he would see me again sometime. And he often did, until his death. His name was John, and he spent a lot of time in cafés where he would be provided with coffee. He picked up newspapers there and free calendars at the bank, and sold them as he could. Almost everyone knew him, spoke to him, and looked out for him.

An emotionally disturbed man who lives alone and by choice in a house without electricity or running water finds a bag of groceries on his porch with regularity. A woman who speaks at every meeting of the school board with good intentions but a poor grasp of the facts is accepted. Such is the value of forbearance in small towns.

> Samuel Johnson said, "A decent provision for the poor is the true test of civilization." Perhaps an even finer one is the way a place treats the mentally ill. A lot of citizens went out of their way to speak to the town's former mental patients. Some downtown merchants joined the cops in looking after them.[18]

Because of their valuing forbearance, small towns often do a good job in caring for the different and the marginalized.

But as noted earlier with regard to community, this forbearance may be more readily extended to individuals than to classes or groups that are different. And there is a limit on how many eccentrics one town can accommodate. Furthermore, the suppression of conflict for the sake of harmony means that skills needed to deal with conflict may not be developed. Thus, when a serious crisis hits a small town, skills and resources may be unavailable to respond creatively and nondestructively. Caring for individuals who are different or in crisis does not always translate to the ability to handle a divisive, community-wide crisis.

> I have observed that in the small town, the need to get along favors the passive aggressives, those for whom honest differences and disagreements pose such a threat that they are quickly submerged, left to fester in a complex web of resentments. This is why, when the tempests do erupt in small towns, they are so violently destructive.[19]

Small-town people's forbearance toward one another is a distinguishing value, but one that may not run deep enough to sustain the community in the face of the large-scale changes many small towns are facing.

These four values—community, longevity, sense of place, forbearance— are characteristic of many small towns, and enable them to create a nourishing quality of life for many. However, failing to address the problems associated with each of these values may put small communities at risk when confronted with change and crises. Understanding both these values and the problems associated with them will enable those ministering in small towns to help them continue to be life-giving places.

> For all its smallness, Northampton had great absorptive powers. The parts mattered less than their combination—geography and history and architecture, workable proportions of human frailty and virtue. If civilization implies more than TVs and dishwashers, more than artistic achievement and wise rule, it implies just this, a place with a life that shelters individual lives, a place that allows people to become better than they might otherwise be—better, in a sense, than they are.[20]

Ministering in the Small Town

CHAPTER 5

Ministerial Role

W hen I first began small-town ministry, a wise and experienced small-town pastor told me, "Remember, no matter how long you stay, you will always be an outsider." This remark was intended not as a discouraging word, but as an instruction on the role of the minister in small towns. "Because secrets are hard to keep and memories are long in small towns, the community needs an outsider who takes confidentiality seriously."[1]

Outsider

Someone is needed beyond the confines of family, neighborhood, and community to whom small-town folk may confide their deepest yearnings, secrets, follies, and fears. Paradoxically, it is by embracing this role, rather than by trying too hard to be accepted as a part of the community, that the small-town minister secures a place in the community. Otherwise, the minister runs the fatal risk of being "too much himself, too small for his position, too anxious to fit into our community, too sweaty and dirty and casual and unwise."[2]

This is not to say that small towns are not hospitable to outsider pastors. They are, just as they are often hospitable to other newcomers at a certain level. But whereas other newcomers can, over time, become an accepted part of the community, pastors are held apart in order to serve their much-needed function. For often in small towns, where so much is known about almost everyone, those struggling with personal problems need someone with whom to talk who will keep private concerns out of the flow of community talk. The parents of a gay child or the gay child himself, the business owner who doesn't want everyone to know she cannot compete with new national retailers, the infertile couple wanting to explore adoption quietly, the farmer fearful of losing a farm that has been in his family for three generations, and any number of others need a trusted outsider able to hold their concerns with compassion and confidentiality. Trying too hard to fit in, to work one's way into the power structure and groups with influence over local affairs, will result in the sacrifice of the small-town minister's unique and essential role of trusted outsider.

Other small-town outsiders may include social workers, psychologists, physicians, teachers, pharmacists, dentists, attorneys[3]—anyone who has skills that are needed and that have been obtained outside the community, and whose work requires confidentiality. It is not uncommon in a small community for practitioners of these professions to end up socializing together. The small-town minister needs to exercise some measure of care here, lest too much separation from the rest of the community be perceived as aloofness, or a sense of elitism be fostered among professionals out of their own sense of not belonging.

Being outsiders necessarily means that it is often more difficult for small-town ministers to form friendships with members of the congregation. Perceptions of favoritism and discomfort with too much closeness can make friendships with parishioners difficult. However, in small communities where there are several churches, rich ecumenical relationships, both social and professional (study or support groups), are often found simply because the ministers need one another's understanding to cope with the feelings of not quite belonging the way long-term residents do. And friendships with folk outside the congregation are certainly acceptable.

The minister-as-outsider can play the important role of connecting small-town people beset by insularity with needed resources outside the community. I have often been surprised that townspeople are unaware of good restaurants in a nearby city and have enjoyed recommending one. But more than this, the tendency toward insularity may keep people unaware of resources that would be of significant help. As an outsider who has taken the time to learn what resources are available in other communities, I have often been able to connect people with therapists or support groups appropriate to needs such as substance-abuse treatment, divorce recovery, or cancer support groups. My accepting the role of trusted outsider means that people will usually trust as worthwhile a resource I recommend.[4]

Small-town folk are often wary, with a caution born of experience, that outsider professionals like ministers will have a short tenure among them. And because they value longevity, it will, as mentioned previously, often take some time before a minister will be invited into positions of community influence. Ministerial skill, training, and experience may all be grounds for respect, but it is the evidence of staying power that usually persuades people that the minister is committed to the town and worthy of a significant role in community organizations. A well-trained and capable minister new to small-town work had trouble understanding why a somewhat ordinary and not very dynamic minister seemed to be on every important committee in town. The reason was simple: He had been in town for more than 20 years, and no other minister had been there more than five. Even in the face of change, small towns seek to be known for what they are and to maintain coherence and continuity with their history. Ministers who stay, and who stay true to their trusted-outsider role, will in time find themselves entrusted with more responsibility in the community.

A paradoxical aspect of the role of minister as outsider is that small-town folk generally desire that their ministers patronize local businesses and use local professional services whenever possible. To the extent possible, it is more than a little prudent for the small-town minister to find a local physician, insurance agent, hair stylist, pharmacist, attorney, and any other service providers needed. Almost everyone will know where these services are being secured, whether in town or elsewhere. Seeking them outside the community conveys the message that the minister is not committed to the community's economic well-being or that local providers are looked down upon as not being good enough. Shopping locally for goods and services quietly but importantly asserts the minister's commitment to the town as home.

The role of trusted outsider does not confine the small-town minister to play only that role. Conceiving of ministry too narrowly and using it as an excuse not to participate in the larger life of the town will undermine the trusted-outsider role. It is necessary, and usually quite enjoyable, to attend such community events as parades and athletic matches. Going to football or basketball or soccer games is not only an opportunity to see the church youth in another setting; it also affirms one's interest in the town as a whole. Such attendance not only is part of the ongoing history-gathering work; it shows the minister's desire to belong as much as is possible within the limits of the outsider role.

Pontifex

In addition to a self-understanding centered on the acceptance of outsider status, the small-town minister may also find helpful the ministerial metaphor of "pontifex"—literally, bridge builder. Besides helping people bridge the distance to resources that lie beyond the community, the small-town minister can do bridge-building within the community. Churches, service clubs, medical facilities, schools, and other groups in a small town may engage in a fair amount of turf protection. This tendency becomes understandable if one realizes that the resources needed for such organizations— volunteers and members, donations of money and materials, media exposure—are in limited supply. When I became involved in a number of such community groups (after several years in town, of course), I noticed that members of one group were sometimes only dimly aware of what was going on in another. Hospital staff might not, for example, know much about school issues, and vice versa. Surprisingly often, I have been able to be a bridge from one group to another—putting people working on similar issues in touch with one another, sharing information, pointing out scheduling conflicts. Because I am an outsider who happens to have his feet in a number of camps and who is not seen as having a particular group's ax to grind, I can be a helpful bridge builder among various groups.[5]

A small-town minister can function out of the pontifex model in other ways. One is to bring to town outsiders who can helpfully interpret the larger world. This is an old tradition of many churches that, for example, have invited missionaries on furlough to speak at a potluck supper about their work in a far-off corner of the world. I once heard the late ecumenical leader Eugene Carson Blake say that until high school, he knew more about the geography of several African countries than he did about that of the United States because of listening for years to such speakers. That tradition can continue in a deepened way, and in a way particularly helpful to the small town confronted with an inbreaking larger world. Most ministers will have contact with resources through denominational or seminary programs that will provide speakers or pastors-in-residence from other regions or countries. Such visitors may not only bring before the town a different perspective on issues; they may share their expertise through short-term assistance on such issues as conflict management. Another possibility is bringing in program leaders— for retreats, choir workshops, adult education events, programs sponsored in cooperation with other organizations—from ethnic groups with which the local community may not yet have much familiarity.

Once a modern dance troupe came to Lemmon [Iowa] to work in the schools. They choreographed a witty dance about tilling the soil and got high school students to perform it. They held a workshop for the football team on avoiding injury and working with damaged muscles. . . . Best of all, the troupe managed to assault a number of racial and social stereotypes held by the young people of Lemmon, whose knowledge of the outer world is severely limited. Much of what they know of other races they get from television cop shows. One dancer was a black man who had been raised on a farm in Indiana and had broken horses for a living. He'd been a bull rider on the rodeo circuit and told the students he'd given it up because it wasn't good for his body. "I'd rather dance," he said, and I felt he'd earned his fee right there.[6]

Again, because the minister has a certain credibility, a bridge can be built between the community and the larger world that allows the realities of the outside world to be experienced in a safe and helpful way.

Finally, the image of small-town minister as pontifex is crucial when reaching out to the poor. Poverty is real and increasing in small communities, and is often somewhat hidden. (See particularly *Broken Heartland*, by Davidson; *Worlds Apart*, by Duncan; and *Out of Sight, Out of Mind*, by Vissing.) While it is easy to see the impact of economic change on farmers forced to sell their land or on small businesses compelled to close, one may overlook members of the underclass who are either unemployed or marginally employed. These people often do not experience themselves as part of the community or of such institutions as its churches. Because they besmirch the romantic ideal of the small town, they are sometimes almost intentionally overlooked or ignored.

Building a relational bridge to such people is important not only in working to meet their material needs, but also in integrating them into the larger life of the community. Speaking from the baptismal understanding of the worth of all people and out of the church's concern for justice, the small-town minister is uniquely positioned to address the various needs of the marginalized. Costs may be associated with such bridge-building. A small-town minister recently told me how he and his family were excluded from the social circle of professionals when they befriended a migrant-worker family that had settled in the community. And yet, because small towns do value community and are able to accommodate those who are different, there are grounds for bridge-building, particularly through a church that understands itself as called to inclusivity.

Community Builder

The minister as community builder serves another important role in small towns. That may seem strange to say, given the importance small towns attach to community. But with changes caused by economic development or deterioration and the accompanying increase or decrease in population, community is no longer a given.[7] Furthermore, dramatic change can cause deep divisions in small towns, depending on who benefits and who suffers.

> Small towns pride themselves on their sense of community, the neighborliness which lack of anonymity is supposed to provide. When everyone knows everyone else, the theory goes, community is highly valued. This is evident when disaster strikes. A farmer hospitalized in early summer finds that his neighbors have put up his hay. A new widow's kitchen fills with friends and acquaintances who bring food, coffee, memories and healing. But the fault line of suspicion and divisiveness exposed by the farm crisis of the mid-1980s has left wounds that have not healed, making me wonder how real community is in my town.[8]

Small towns do value community and are usually highly skilled at coping with a crisis in an individual's or family's life. But systemic changes caused by forces not subject to local control are often more than small-town coping mechanisms can handle. Large-scale change can rend the fabric of small-town life, and it is this fact that necessitates the minister's continuing efforts at community-building. Loss of economic viability and therefore one's place in the community or the arrival of many newcomers from different ethnic groups or social classes can shatter the sense of belonging, a sense so long in place and accepted that people may have no notion of how to recreate it.

It is well to remember that Jesus' very first act of ministry was to call the disciples—in other words, to create a community. This point suggests that the creation of community should be a primary activity of the minister, particularly in a small town. When I served in a suburban context, I spent a great deal of energy seeking to build community in the congregation, designing events to deepen relationships and develop the sense of belonging to one another in Christ. Much of this expenditure was in vain, I came to realize, because people often move to suburbs for privacy and not because they value community. Quite a different situation prevails in small communities. Here, belonging to one another, relating to one another is, as I have noted, a core value. Those activities that enhance the sense of belonging and of community will be embraced. I was surprised to see how warmly received, without objection, was a program in which women explored and experienced alternative images of God. In a relatively traditional congregation, I thought, at the very least, eyebrows would be raised. However, not a word was said against the program for the simple reason that it deepened community.[9]

The building of community begins in worship. In small towns, the minister as worship leader needs to call forth the gifts of the congregation as musicians, liturgists, lay preachers, and so forth. Specific naming of pastoral concerns—births, illnesses, deaths, marriages, achievements—should be part of worship, particularly the lifting up of these in prayer. Small-town congregations "usually do not need to be reorganized or programmed as much as they need to be appreciated, affirmed, encouraged, equipped and challenged."[10] And this needs to happen in worship. Active attention should be given to newcomers as the church practices inclusiveness, proclaiming its welcome of those who may not be welcome elsewhere. Worship need not be "dumbed down," as Marva Dawn puts it, but it must be personal in the small town. Preaching needs to interweave the biblical narratives with the narrative of the town where possible, and must avoid abstraction and generality. Small-town folk assume that God is at work in the world but long to have that belief named within the context of their life experience.[11] And because they are closely attuned to the rhythms of the seasons, they are often remarkably open to liturgical emphasis on the church year. Furthermore, in a season of great change in so many small towns, it is important to convey hope and God's power to bring new life out of death to empower people to live in a world that may be quite different from the one long known, stable, and cherished.[12]

Emphasizing community in worship leads to the expansion of community-building activities both within (as noted above) and beyond the congregation. The small-town minister can initiate and demonstrate a habit of listening to the town to discern what needs the church may address. Perhaps the church can help bring together those in the community who seek to monitor the conversion of agricultural land or environmentally sensitive land into residential development; or to provide an after-school program for children whose parents must now commute to work; or to spearhead the securing of a medical clinic; or to help establish a Habitat for Humanity program to provide decent housing as a way out of poverty.

Community is what small towns often used to specialize in. And community is what the church is and does. Ministerial leadership needs to focus on healing the brokenness of small towns where it exists and on continually building up the shared relational life both within and beyond the congregation.

Town Type Influence

The type of town—Mighthavebeenville, Agraville, Ribbonville, or Fairview (see chapter 1)—can be decisive for the role the minister needs to assume. Perhaps the most difficult situation is in a Mighthavebeenville that has no prospects for survival, let alone growth. Here the minister may have to function much like a hospice chaplain, companioning a dying church and community. This is not work for the fainthearted, but it is an essential work of ministry, as people must find new life elsewhere after the death of their town.

Furthermore, in some situations the general rule of staying in place as an outsider for a considerable length of time before seeking to influence public life may not apply. In Fairviews where a means of surviving (e.g., resort development, retirement community, prison construction) has been found, or in a Ribbonville being rapidly encroached upon economically and demographically by a nearby city, residents may need the leadership skills a minister brings to help manage the change and accompanying conflict. The situation may be sufficiently dynamic that it is not possible to take all the time needed to settle in and learn the community before stepping in and offering leadership. Such might also be the case in a Mighthavebeenville that finds itself with an economic opportunity to help it survive, but lacks the skills to ensure that change does not cause so much upheaval and dislocation that the town loses its uniqueness. The small-town minister, acting out of concern for those most likely to be hurt by change or with an outsider's appreciation of the historical character of the town, may be able to ask important questions to ameliorate some of the less desirable or even painful aspects wrought by inevitable change. In such a situation, an unwillingness to exert community leadership for the sake of pastoral concerns within the church can result in a tragic failure.

Trusted outsider, builder of bridges within the community and to the larger world, developer of community within the church and the town, as well as any number of specialized functions required by the particular context— truly the ministerial role is a complex one in small communities. Committing oneself strongly to confidentiality, working always to connect people with resources and one another, not taking too much to oneself, and accepting those functions the community needs and cannot provide for itself will all enhance ministerial effectiveness. Lack of these will do quite the opposite. Careful exegesis of the small-town context will ensure that the needed ministerial roles are rightly understood and can therefore be embraced.

CHAPTER 6

Pastoral Care

P astoral care in the small-town church can be most rewarding, particularly if the minister understands what type of care is most warranted. Typically, small-town churches have strong networks for support of members. These networks readily supply food, visits, cards, and transportation in times of need. It is not at all uncommon for meals to be brought to a family with a seriously ill member night after night for months on end. Or rides to a nearby city where needed ongoing therapy is available will be arranged for as long as needed. Often a church member, whether or not a member of the congregation's official compassion committee, will take the initiative to organize the needed help, even without a request from the pastor. The support network provides as well the listening ears of trusted friends who have long been part of the person's life.

"Priestly Care"

All of this care tends to free the small-town minister to provide what others cannot provide, and that might be called "priestly care." By priestly care, I mean to draw emphasis to the minister's role in praying with those in need and bearing the sacraments to them. While care must be taken not to become simply the official sayer of prayers, small-town people look to and deeply value the minister as the one who prays with and for them. Most others in the support network will not do this work, seeing it as within the purview of the minister. A minister new to a small town and much shaped by her clinical pastoral education (CPE) experience in a hospital was glad to exercise her considerable listening skills when visiting the sick. But she quickly got the message that what members in need desired was her priestly work when three parishioners in a row asked during an afternoon of visitation, "Are we going to pray now?" Being the one "who prayed for me" at home or in the hospital or during worship, the one who brought Holy Communion, who gathered the family for a service of healing at home (or church), is the distinctive contribution of the small-town minister in the small-town church support network.

Another aspect of priestly care has to do with the minister's work at baptisms, funerals, and weddings. Because small-town residents place a high value on belonging to and being known by the community, these occasions cannot simply be done "by the book" but need to be personalized to name the distinctive character and gifts of those involved in the rites. It is through preparation with individuals and families for these turning points in life's journey that the minister comes to belong most deeply to the community, albeit within the confines of being the trusted outsider. Baptisms that celebrate the new disciple by name and family lineage (and perhaps the history and meaning of the name); weddings that tell of the journey the couple has made in the community as well as the special gifts each partner brings to the vocation of marriage; and funerals in which the deceased's life is lifted up honestly, wholly, and gratefully—these are among the most important moments in small-town ministry. They are the times when the minister, so often and necessarily an outsider, most belongs.

An essential part of the small-town minister's pastoral work is the integration of those who are not yet part of existing support networks. The assimilation of newcomers into church life is a high priority and a highly visible aspect of the minister's work. Being a newcomer to a town and a congregation can be difficult enough without the loneliness incurred in a time of need when no one responds. And with more people moving to small towns in many areas, this ministry is a widespread need. Helping people become integrated into church life happens, of course, in formal and informal ways. Formal programs of pairing newcomers with old-timers; of systematically bringing new people into classes, small groups, choirs, and committees; and of making the day of reception into membership a highlight of worship—all are good ways of helping to structure such integration. Getting newcomers involved in the giving end of care networks will help them become known and appreciated before the time comes when they need to be on the receiving end. Furthermore, in most churches, a few members are gifted with an appropriately extroverted sense of welcome.

If the small-town minister will do but a little work to help folk see the use of this gift as a much-needed ministry within the congregation to help new people become part of the community, much of the work of integration can be accomplished quickly and naturally.

Counseling

Stress is caused by change. With the many changes, good and bad, coming to small communities, it is not surprising to find much stress and its concomitant effects. Substance abuse, depression and suicide, family violence, stress-related accidents and illnesses are all common problems.[1] And often, the resources to address these matters, though readily available in urban and suburban settings, are not so easily found in small towns. Furthermore, small-town people may fail to make use of available resources out of a sense of rugged individualism or a desire to keep problems as private as possible. A troubled parishioner may not want people to see his car parked at the church on a regular basis.[2]

The counseling aspect of pastoral care can be both important and difficult to implement in the small town. In contrast to urban and suburban settings, where the minister usually has a number of mental-health professionals to whom referrals can be made, it is more likely that the need for counseling in small towns will fall, in some part if not largely, on the minister. One needs counseling skills, and these skills need continuing development as specific needs in the community are identified. Furthermore, the small-town minister needs to be creative in making the opportunities for counseling. Rather than waiting in the office for people to show up, one must take more initiative to go where the troubled people are. Initial contacts with a troubled person might take place in a farmyard, on a back porch, in the back room of a shop, or on a walk. To a certain extent, this approach flies in the face of pastoral training that advocates letting the initiative lie with the client rather than the counselor. But in ten years of approaching on their turf the parishioners I believed to be troubled (rather than inviting them to come by the office to talk sometime), I have been rebuffed only once. Word will spread of the minister's ability as a counselor. It is not necessary to advertise. And some parishioners will initiate contact for needed help. But more often than not in the small community, the minister will have to make the first move.

The question then becomes how to know whom to approach. Listening, the key to history-taking, is also key here.

> Experience indicates that the fine art of listening is central to understanding [small] communities. Listening is best done on the front porch, over a cup of coffee at the town diner or feed mill, at Little League games, and all the other casual places where town and country folk tend to gather.[3]

In these contexts (and others like the service-station pump, the church door after worship, in the parking lot after a meeting) the gentle pleas for help will be heard by those ministers who have ears to hear. But the offer of help must be extended in private and on the home turf of the one in need.

If a problem (e.g., substance abuse, depression over job loss) is found to be afflicting numbers of people, it may be possible in time to create a support network among them, or even a relatively formal support group. But this must be done slowly and with absolute consistency in asking permission of the troubled person to be put in contact with others sharing similar struggles. The lack of anonymity in small towns (the smaller the town, the greater this lack) makes it essential to help people "save face." Failure to respect people in this way will not only further harm the hurting; it will cripple the minister's credibility. "But I was only trying to help" is never an acceptable excuse.

Boundaries

Multiple-generation and extended families are not at all uncommon in small towns. And this fact has two implications for ministry. First, it is important for the minister to take the time to understand kinship patterns. Woe to the pastor who makes an offhand and less-than-flattering remark about someone outside the congregation, only to learn that the individual in question is a cousin or in-law of a parishioner! More important, congregational boundaries tend to be rather porous in small-town churches, and often many members of an extended family will be considered "members" of a church even though they have never joined and attend only sporadically. The small-town minister will often be asked to officiate at weddings, funerals, and baptisms of people he has never met but who are considered part of the church.

Thus, as far as permitted by particular denominational polity, the small-town minister will find his ministry reaching into the community at large on many occasions.

It should be noted that one way to increase the size of many a small-town church is to endeavor to deepen the commitment of these "nonmember members" so that they will become more than de facto parts of the congregation. On more than one occasion such people have told me that they had never joined the church simply because they had never been asked. It was not so much that they wanted the benefits the church offers without making a commitment as that the status quo of their relationship had simply been accepted by the congregation and its ministers.

But, as previously mentioned, boundaries can be quite strict in small towns, particularly those of class and ethnicity. Where these do not comport with the Gospel, they must be challenged. I have often found that small-town church members are not comfortable with such negative boundaries in social arrangements, that they know such divisions are not right, and yet are unsure of what to do about them. And, of course, no easy solutions to these matters are evident in small towns any more than in urban or suburban areas. But often, gently naming the problem of these boundaries will give congregations permission to wrestle with them, and stimulate innovative ways of beginning to overcome them.

One caution in this regard has to do with racially and ethnically based churches in small towns. While shared services on special occasions like Thanksgiving or Martin Luther King, Jr., Day or shared vacation Bible school programs or invitations to one another's fellowship events can be beneficial, honest respect for the integrity of congregations of other racial and ethnic groups is essential. One African-American pastor put it to me this way: "Everything we can do to help people get along in day-to-day community life, we must do. But you must realize that the church is the only social institution we control in this town. It is our power base in the community, and must remain so."

If small-town church boundaries are porous, the minister needs to make her own boundaries clear. This not only means understanding her role clearly; it means setting limits on work time. Because ministers bump into members all the time in small towns—at the grocery store, in the bank, while getting a haircut, or having dinner at a restaurant—a strong tendency persists to be "on" (that is, in work mode) all the time. This availability is part of what makes small-town ministry so demanding and not an escape from the rigors of the suburban or urban church. Making clear when one is going to be at the church for routine administrative work and when one is going to be out calling or working on sermon preparation will help, as will clarity about time reserved for one's family. It is also advisable to make known one's day off, and even to get out of town, if possible, for that day. It's hard to hide at home in a small town, and getting away is often the best way to renew oneself for the somewhat relentless dailiness of small-town ministry.

Self-Care

"Who pastors the pastor?" is an important question for all ministers to ask themselves. Too often, the answer is "no one," and the pastor is isolated and despairing, or the answer is "the pastor's family"—a situation that leaves the members feeling burdened. Caring for the self is essential for the small-town minister for the reasons noted: lack of privacy, being "on" almost all the time, being an outsider, not having shared as deeply as many in the long history of the place. Thus, intentional self-care is crucial for the small-town minister.

Relationships with other small-town clergy, as I have observed, can be a helpful part of self-care. These are people in the same boat, who have experienced the demands of small-town ministry. If the town is so small that it has only one church or if there is competitiveness among the churches (as sometimes happens over doctrinal differences or attempts to increase membership at almost any cost), then it may be best to seek out the companionship of ministers from nearby small towns. Such gatherings should be regular, at least monthly and perhaps as often as weekly, and can be designed simply for fellowship or centered on study and spiritual growth, or combine some of each.

Taking time for continuing-education events is another meaningful aspect of self-care. Some members may resist this use of the pastor's time, saying, "We don't get to do that. Why should she?" But if it is made clear that continuing-education time is used to strengthen skills useful in the small-town context (counseling skills appropriate to a recurring need among parishioners, handling change or conflict, perhaps even small-town economic development), such resistance can be overcome. Plans for continuing education need to be shared with, and endorsed by, church governing boards. And the longer a minister stays in a particular town, the more support she will receive for continuing education, since the community will benefit by it. In addition, such events usually afford some time away from the intensity of small-town life.

Another educational component of self-care has to do with keeping up academically and ecclesiastically with the larger world through journals and books (and also the Internet). I have encountered too many small-town clergy who have apparently succumbed to a certain inertia and to the insularity of their context, and no longer study. So much good material is available on every aspect of ministry (and so much of it on the Internet) that this is a regrettable, and sometimes self-destructive, choice. It is a failure to bridge to the larger world, not only for the benefit of one's church, but also for oneself.

Isolation as a problem of small-town ministry can also be addressed by serving in denominational capacities that afford involvement with others. Two kinds of difficulties may be encountered here. First, some parishioners may see such involvements as unnecessary time away from town. And second, small-town ministers often come face to face with the lack of understanding of their context when working with urban and suburban ministers. Nevertheless, the change can be refreshing, and sometimes a source of new ideas and possibilities for small-town ministry. Denominations may become more attentive to the unique needs of small-town ministry through the service of small-town ministers (and their persistent raising of small-town issues as distinctive from urban and suburban ones) on denominational committees, boards, and councils.

Small towns are often wonderful places for the care of the physical self. While there may be no health clubs nearby, opportunities for outdoor recreation—walking, running, biking, cross-country skiing—abound, and usually in beautiful settings. In fact, the natural beauty of small-town settings—sunsets easily seen, storms whose approach can be watched sometimes for hours, astonishing night skies, all manner of seasonal fragrances borne on the wind—can be nourishing and healing for those who take the time to engage them. Availing oneself of these possibilities can be nothing less than life-giving.

CHAPTER 7

Congregational Role and Ministry

L ike the settings in which they are found, small-town churches are communities of memory. Most have long and well-established traditions that have bestowed identity on the people for many years, through many changes. The central issue in these congregations is the balance between the preservation and continuation of these traditions and the cultivation of new possibilities in ministry. Neither a rigid adherence to the old nor an uncritical embrace of the new will serve the small-town church well. The balance needed in the church mirrors that which is needed in the community as a whole, and indeed, the church can sometimes demonstrate a life-giving balance as the small town is confronted with change.

Small-town churches are often remarkable for their refusal to die. Even when the town is stagnant or declining and the church's membership is steadily aging, members will stubbornly hang on, as many a church bureaucrat has discovered when endeavoring to close or merge a church without having done a thorough job of understanding the church and its context. This clinging to life can, however, be channeled into new ministries to ensure the future by ministerial leadership committed to learning and honoring the church's story.

It should also be noted that while churches of various sizes can be found in small towns (there are even small-town churches that model themselves on urban megachurches), smaller congregations with less than 100 in worship each Sunday are most common, particularly in Mighthavebeenville, Agraville, and Fairview towns. Usually these congregations cannot be "full-service" churches offering everything in the way of programming from music to education to youth work to fellowship activities. Thus, small-town congregations will often specialize in some aspect of congregational life. In asking how churches are perceived in the community (see chapter 2), one commonly hears comments that make clear, for example, that the Methodists are known for their music program, while the Congregationalists have lots of small groups for adults and the Lutherans have a great youth program. Doing a few activities well is usually more important than straining limited resources to have every kind of program available.

Small-town churches confronted with change have essentially three choices: Do nothing, change the church, or change the community. It has been suggested that people in small communities, having weathered many storms in the past, may be tempted to choose the first option—taking a wait-and-see position.[1] After all, they have survived for a long time and have seen other institutions come and go. But the scale of change confronting small towns and the pervasive impact of mass culture and the Information Age make the choice to do nothing increasingly less tenable. In truth, it may be the death knell of some small towns, particularly Mighthavebeenvilles.

A more creative response is a context-appropriate blend of changing the church and working to change the community. Because the church and community live in such dynamic relationship with each other in the small town, both types of change are warranted. Jeremiah's words ring true today for the small-town church and its community: "Seek the welfare of the city where I have sent you . . . and pray on its behalf, for in its welfare you will find your welfare" (Jer.25:7).

Role and Ministry According to Need

In every context, small-town churches should assess what needs exist in their community which they are called by God to meet according to the gifts of the congregation. Not unlike small-town businesses confronted with competition from large retailers, they need to find a niche market not being served, both to have a focus beyond themselves and to enhance life for the town. Many of the changes impinging on small communities have already been suggested—economic challenges due to changes in traditional activities like farming and the arrival of national franchises; growing ethnic diversity; decrease of public-assistance programs for the poor in many areas; consolidation of schools and government services; influx of newcomers for retirement, recreation, or work based in the home; changes in work patterns. Each of these creates stresses and needs within the small town. As a first step toward establishing new ministries, churches need to assess what needs are not being met.

The needs of the poor will be part of the picture in almost every small town. Dislocated workers, families deep in debt, migrant laborers, hourly wage earners with few or no benefits, and single-parent households are but some of the poor. Assistance programs for basic needs such as food, shelter, and utilities are often needed. But just as essential are programs to integrate the poor into the social institutions of the community—schools and churches among them. Churches may want to investigate health clinics to provide the vaccinations children need to go to school, or mentoring programs or latchkey children's programs that include Christian education and music.

In a time of shrinking government involvement in social services, a small-town church may discover populations of need not being helped. A congregation might establish a program for pregnant teens or teen mothers if few resources are available for this group. Only a few young women may be in need, but the small numbers are often just right for a small church to work with, perhaps pairing young mothers with church grandmothers whose children and grandchildren have moved away. Drawing these people in need into the church family will benefit both.

The needs of the aging in small towns are real, but the population may not be served by the resources available in large communities. Options to explore might include parish nurse programs, help with taxes or Social Security matters, a service to provide minor home repairs, as well as various social groups or meal programs. But the need of the aging to contribute is essential to their well-being. The independent-minded small-town older person cannot be put in a class of those who only receive; they must be able to give out of their experience as well.

A congregation with concerns for environmental matters might look to start a recycling program for its town as part of a program on stewardship of the land. A church in a community where migrant workers are employed might explore the need for day care or translators or an athletic program for youth. A church with members skilled in computer use might offer classes on the uses of the Internet for small businesses. A congregation with a mentally impaired young person might begin a Christian education program for all such folk in town.

Because of the wide variety of small contexts, it is difficult to generalize about role and ministry, so such possibilities are intended to be suggestive. However, in general, the small-town church can serve the community by helping it wrestle with a change in its historic functioning, by seeking to encourage appropriate development, and by ministering to those who are hurting because of changes in the town.

> In some places you will feel a need to get change started. In other places you may feel a need to guide, even put the brakes on runaway change. A few will need to help communities deal with life-threatening decline; others may help the community through a change of direction and focus; and still others may lead through the changes that come with becoming a different size. . . . Draw upon the biblical principles of justice and love to analyze the changes occurring. . . . Guard against discrimination, environmental [degradation], exploitation of workers, political corruption, and growing poverty.[2]

A more demanding task facing small-town congregations is that of helping people confront systemic injustices before which they feel powerless. While meeting specific local needs is important work to which small-town churches are called, it cannot be denied that in many places hate groups have arisen because people feel they have lost control over much of their lives to forces that have treated them unjustly.

> The widespread sense of powerlessness and loss of control that many rural [and small-town] people feel as well as the genuine injustices that they have undergone have focused rage against a cluster of targets, with the federal government and its agents being the most visible and easily accessible. It would be a mistake for the church to simply decry the violence that these groups practice or occasion without recognizing as well the precipitating injustice that cause[s] these people to cry out.[3]

If the church does not respond to the real grievances of people in small towns, if it retreats into a spirituality disconnected from the genuine concerns of community members, it is in danger of becoming "a tradition bypassed"[4] and a resource irrelevant to its context. At the very least, the small-town congregation must be honest in naming the forces working against the best interests of its community so that community members will not readily seek out other, and finally fruitless, ways of sharing their pain. What is needed are small-town congregations that take seriously the sense of

outrage among people victimized by change while offering constructive alternatives to the expression of that outrage.

Another large-scale problem confronting small communities previously
dependent on agriculture is environmental degradation.

> [T]he transformation of farming into an agribusiness has brought
> with it a host of environmental problems, including ground water
> depletion and contamination, soil toxification, and contamination of
> food supplies. These facts surprise many of us, especially since
> we see the abundance of food in the supermarkets created by
> agribusiness. But this abundance comes at a very high cost and
> with a skewed accounting system. Agribusiness depends on cheap
> oil and an unlimited supply of water and soil. These conditions
> cannot last. We are transferring to future generations the prob-
> lems of coping with an exhausted soil and contaminated water
> supply. The sins of the fathers will be visited upon the children.[5]

But since the scale of this problem is great and its consequences in the
future (though perhaps the not-too-distant future), it is difficult to address,
and may only give rise either to a frustration of powerlessness or to a kind
of despair that says nothing can be done as the community watches the
former basis of its life deteriorate. Here, a challenging paradox of small-
town ministry comes clear: Leadership needs to be adept at handling the
intricacies of small organizations and at the same time skilled at empower-
ing those organizations to cope with enormous issues seemingly beyond
their control but surely impinging upon them. Perhaps one of the most important roles a small-town church can play is to build networks with other
such churches to begin to develop the skills needed to face such large issues systematically and hopefully.

Using the Internet, for example, to link with other communities and
organizations seeking to cope with the negative impact of many current
agricultural practices may well help people overcome feelings of powerlessness and begin to find alternatives and restorative farming methods.
Internet connections may also assist in overcoming the small town's feeling
of isolation in confronting large-scale problems and the institutions responsible for them.

Role and Ministry According to Town Type

The challenges of ministry in Mighthavebeenville churches are great, and are often dealt to recent seminary graduates. Mighthavebeenvilles are imperiled in part because they have tended to be single-function communities.[6] If the town is indeed heading toward dissolution, and with it the church, then "dying with dignity" may need to be the overriding goal. If that is not the case, then the development of a focused ministry will be essential to the congregation. Mighthavebeenville churches may need to become what have been called "signature churches"—churches whose identity is shaped by their responsiveness to a need or opportunity in their area. A ministry to home-schooled children, a gospel band, a much-needed Alcoholics Anonymous group have all served in the creation of such signature churches.[7] Maybe the church will begin a historic preservation project or create a community-wide festival for the town. Maybe the community needs a fellowship group for an increasing number of single people in town. Perhaps the congregation will become active in helping to convert the town into a Fairview by helping to secure a government service installation or to locate a developer to construct a retirement community. Second-career ministers who have previously worked in business may be particularly helpful in this setting by "evok[ing] the entrepreneurial gifts of persons"[8] that could help the town find a new economic base.

Mighthavebeenville churches will often need to cooperate with other churches in town to provide activities like vacation Bible school and outreach services like food banks. And it may be in their best interest to forge a bond with a church of the same denomination in another community, perhaps the nearest Agraville or Ribbonville, that would help strengthen its prospects for survival through shared programming and resources. Many Mighthavebeenville churches will survive out of sheer stubbornness; but with vision and creative leadership, they can do more than that and may even help their towns to thrive. Furthermore, cooperative arrangements for ministry may allow the financial resources for supporting a minister to become available, thereby reducing the turnover rate for Mighthavebeenville clergy and contributing to the stability of the churches and their towns.

In Mighthavebeenvilles, more than in the other types of small towns, attention may very well need to be given to establishing some form of cooperative ministry.[9] Such consideration often generates conflict; it cannot be done hastily without much time allowed for both formal and informal discussion of a variety of possible cooperative arrangements. Multichurch parishes in which governance and staff are shared among several churches, yoked parishes in which two churches in two Mighthavebeenvilles share a pastor, or a cluster group of churches in a Mighthavebeenville that gather to share a mission project are all alternatives worth considering.[10] Many denominations offer helpful resources and processes for exploring such alternatives.[11] But the impulse for such an arrangement must come primarily from the Mighthavebeenville church with no hint that it is a solution being imposed from the outside. And such alternatives can be embraced best when they are understood as an opportunity not only to survive, but also to expand ministry beyond the barest of essentials into something more reflective of the baptismal call to service to others in the name of Christ.

Churches in Agravilles—towns which by virtue of major retailers or new industry or the consolidation of government services have become regional service centers—are often confronted with significant economic changes. And, as might be expected, these bring winners and losers. Part of the Agraville church's role is to monitor these changes—to ask at what price development is occurring in terms of the environment and land use; to see which businesses and town residents are being hurt and how they can be helped; and to maintain relationships with churches in Mighthavebeenvilles (which many Agravilles used to be) not undergoing economic transformation. Traditional patterns of work and worship may be changing in Agravilles (new shifts, telecommuters, Sunday employment[12]), requiring creativity on the church's part as it seeks to reach out to people whose time is shaped by such new patterns. Agraville churches can grow not only because the community may be growing, but also by reaching out to those not served by traditional patterns of church life.

Agraville churches may want to encourage their members to become active participants on governmental decision-making bodies such as town councils, planning commissions, zoning boards, and school boards. This participation reflects a commitment to managing and guiding change rather than hunkering down trying to hold out against it. Because demographic changes often accompany economic changes (e.g., an influx of new racial and ethnic groups), Agraville churches may want to explore satellite ministries to support fellowship groups from these groups new to the community until they are able to form a congregation. These satellite groups might use the church's facilities until they become self-sufficient.[13] And Agraville churches may well be challenged to incorporate new members into their formal and informal networks of caring and compassion.

Cooperative ministries among Agraville churches are important both to meet community-wide needs (such as support for the poor) and to continue to nourish community cohesiveness in times of rapid change (through such activities as community-wide worship services). However, not all churches in an Agraville will want to work together. Some ethnic churches with a strong denominational identity and a long-established presence in the community may choose to cling steadfastly to their identity. And new churches may be forming in Agravilles that have no wish to work with others that they view as competititors.

The considerable variety of Fairviews (resort, retirement, prison, military base, college, and artist colony) make for a wide array of contexts in which Fairview churches function, too many to speak to here. Often Fairviews are Mighthavebeenvilles that have been converted from their original function. Accordingly, almost always an "us and them" mentality prevails to a greater or lesser degree—"us" being the small-town residents whose roots and experience extend back before the town's transformation, and "them" being those who have caused the change or have come because of it. "Them" might include vacationers, retirees, new business owners, service personnel, college students, prison staff, or artists. The presence of "them" may also be a seasonal phenomenon.

Such a demographic reality means that many Fairview churches find themselves functioning according to an unusual annual cycle (their busy time may be when most places are slowed down for summer) and seeking to serve both an indigenous group and a seasonal group of participants in the life of the church. Those who visit seasonally may be more affluent than the locals and bring with them a different, and easily resented, set of expectations for church life. The locals, on the other hand, may feel called to preserve some of what used to be distinctive about the community prior to its change, and to share that history with the newcomers or seasonal people. Even if Fairview churches choose not to close themselves off to the newcomers, their ability to exercise the ministry of hospitality may be sorely tested. Developing a welcoming community while preserving a heritage is not easily done.

A further division in a Fairview may be of the "have and have-not" variety, the "haves" being affluent visitors or new residents or those profiting from whatever new economic base has been established, and the "have-nots" being those longer-term residents who have seen their property values and taxes rise, or low-paid workers in the service industry.[14] While programming may need to be flexible to accommodate the schedules of working-class people, it is important that the church not unwittingly create further divisions thereby. The Fairview church will be challenged to create a community where both groups can meet, perhaps establishing the only place in town where that can happen with everyone on a more-or-less-equal footing. The task of becoming a faith community where the rather sharp distinctions of the town itself are overcome is both essential and difficult, and a distinctive calling of the Fairview congregation. Fairview towns may also be places where satellite ministries can be formed to meet the needs of newcomers who are both service workers and members of an ethnic group not present previously.

One potential problem in Fairviews (as well as in rapidly changing Agravilles and Ribbonvilles) is that conflict will ensue between those once accustomed to providing leadership in the community and newcomers seeking to become influential in the decision-making process. Fighting decisions out on a partisan, win-lose basis is detrimental to the quality of small-town life. An important contribution the church can make in such a situation is both to exemplify and recommend decision-making processes that incorporate representatives from both the longtime residents and the newcomers.[15]

Churches in Ribbonvilles are most likely living in a context of more rapid change than other small towns. In fact, they may well be headed toward becoming suburban churches in the near future. Faced with increasing diversity in population, the congregation may experience severe strains in its historic self-understanding. Trying to maintain a small-town identity may, in time, be little more than an exercise in nostalgia and do little to contribute to a vital identity in the future. But as in Fairview churches, it may be important to share what was in Ribbonville before all the change took place. Some newcomers may come to cherish that history and work to preserve some sense of it for the future.

Carving out a new identity for the congregation may often be a focus of Ribbonville church experience. It is possible that urban churches are looking at the town as a possible site for relocation or that denominational officials will see the town as prime territory for a new congregation.[16] Not only is there a considerable influx of new people; there are also likely to be new churches. Newcomers with a different theological perspective from that which has previously prevailed may cause conflict within Ribbonville congregations.[17] Or a division may occur in the community between new churches for new people and old churches for long-term residents.

If a Ribbonville church chooses to reach out to the various newcomers, it will have to be very intentional about new-member assimilation in a competitive church environment. In any event, helping long-term residents cope with the large degree of change—through pastoral care, efforts to keep history alive, active discussion of what the church feels called to be in the future—will be an important task of the Ribbonville church. And here, as elsewhere, attention to how the land and the people are being hurt by change that benefits some, but not all, is crucial. Development may tend to "run away" in Ribbonvilles, and the church can have a significant role in voicing concerns for land and people that would otherwise be lost.

Ribbonville churches may experience dramatic growth in numbers, and the accompanying challenges of such growth—the need for new facilities, additional worship services, more staff. And while these are often seen as nice problems to have, they raise questions of how to ensure continuity between old and new, between cherished traditions and contemporary needs. Church conflict can erupt as surely around these matters as around issues of cooperative ministry in Mighthavebeenville churches, and leadership will be required to manage such conflict creatively. Great and lingering pain may beset those who feel that they have lost not only their town but their church as well, as a Ribbonville changed. The delicate balance between honoring the past and embracing a faithful future is difficult to maintain in all small towns, but perhaps nowhere more difficult than in those places that are leaving the small-town identity behind.

The variety among small towns as well as the variety of churches found therein makes generalizing about forms of ministry difficult. However, the meeting of needs both within and without the congregation will everywhere be important both to the church's vitality and the town's. Ministries born of attentiveness to the particular town type and context will be most likely to flourish.

Recently, a group of Ku Klux Klansmen requested and received a permit to stage a demonstration in the town where I live. The town's response was remarkable and telling. With only three weeks to respond to this intrusion into a small community with a racial-minority population between 10 percent and 15 percent, the community mobilized itself rapidly and creatively. Leaders from across the community, from a wide range of organizations, churches, and businesses, gathered to discuss ways of meeting this challenge. Free and open discussion prevailed, and a range of opinions was expressed. Participants voiced willingness to use the Internet to learn from the experience of other towns confronted with similar demonstrations. Quickly it was realized that the Klan would benefit most if any violence occurred in which its members could claim to be innocent victims seeking to exercise their First Amendment rights. But the greatest concern was centered on how to express to the children and youth of the community that our town was not about racism and hatred.

In the succeeding three weeks, an alternative event was planned, a "Celebration of Diversity Day," at which children and youth of all backgrounds in the community could gather to skateboard, in-line skate, play basketball, swim, and play games. Refreshments, T-shirts, and staff were provided by businesses and concerned citizens. There was music and dancing, and people of all ages showed up and had a great time being together at a site quite some distance from where the Klan was spouting its message of hatred and racism. Although the permit allowed a demonstration of two hours, the Klan left after about 40 minutes, having had for an audience mostly a large contingent of law-enforcement officers and representatives of various media looking for a story. The real story for the town was taking place at the "Celebration of Diversity," where participants successfully turned the Klan's presence into a positive reinforcement of the town's identity. How wonderfully ironic that the hooded Klansmen who wanted to keep their identity secret unwittingly created the opportunity for the community to renew its clarity about, and commitment to, its identity.

It is moments such as this that make small towns such interesting and rewarding places in which to minister. The possibility of living in meaningful community is again and again realized—not perfectly, not without cost, but in ways that are usually life-giving and that provide an alternative to the excesses of autonomy so often seen as the desired goals of mass culture. Caring and compassion are expressed at a human level in small communities. When the mentally handicapped young man who enthusiastically leads the football team onto the field at every home game is absent, people are immediately concerned to know if he is all right. When a family is confronted with medical bills beyond its financial resources, fund-raisers are planned and supported to help out.

The challenges now confronting small towns are often of a larger scale than those of even the fairly recent past; some stem from forces well beyond the scope of local control. Nevertheless, ministers who work to understand what shapes small-town life and how small towns work will, I believe, be able to make significant and creative contributions in helping to preserve what makes these places special, even in the face of such challenges. Not only can ministers who understand the dynamics of small towns lead their churches in strengthening the town; they are often uniquely placed to lend perspective and leadership to the town itself, helping it live out of its cherished history, culture, values, and traditions while finding new ways to respond and survive amid the challenges of the world beyond its boundaries.

Introduction

1. Cited in Berton Roueche, *Special Places: In Search of Small Town America* (Boston: Little Brown, 1982), v.

2. Kathleen Norris, *Dakota: A Spiritual Geography* (New York: Ticknor & Fields, 1993), 165.

3. United States Bureau of the Census, *Statistical Abstract of the United States: 1998* (Washington, D.C., 1998), 46.

4. Shannon Jung and others, *Rural Ministry: The Shape of the Renewal to Come* (Nashville: Abingdon, 1998), 58-60.

5. U.S. Bureau of the Census, *Statistical Abstract*, 46.

6. Jung, *Rural Ministry*, 108.

7. Kenneth M. Johnson and Calvin L. Beale, "The Rural Rebound Revisited," *American Demographics* 17:7 (July 1995): 46.

8. Johnson and Beale, "Rural Rebound," 48.

9. Tom Morganthau and others, "America's Small Town Boom," *Newsweek* 98:1 (July 6, 1981): 27.

10. David McCullough, Introduction to David Plowden, *Small Town America* (New York: Harry N. Abrams, 1994), 6.

11. John C. Allen and Don A. Dillman, *Against All Odds: Rural Community in the Information Age* (Boulder: Westview Press, 1994), 210.

12. McCullough, Introduction, 4.

13. McCullough, Introduction, 5.

Chapter 1: Geography

1. Emilia E. Martinez-Brawley, *Perspectives on the Small Community: Humanistic Views for Practitioners* (Silver Spring, Md.: National Association of Social Workers Press, 1990), 169.

2. Wayne Franklin and Michael Steiner, "Taking Place: Toward the Regrounding of American Studies," in Wayne Franklin and Michael Steiner, eds., *Mapping American Culture* (Iowa City: University of Iowa Press, 1992), 5.

3. R. Alex Sim, *Land and Community* (Guelph, Ontario: University of Guelph, 1988). This book is out of print and difficult to locate. A good working summary of Sim's approach can be found in Jung, *Rural Ministry.* Another very helpful small-town classification scheme is that of Fred E. H. Schroeder, "Types of American Small Towns and How to Read Them," *Southern Quarterly* 19:1 (fall 1980): 104-135.

4. Drake Hokanson, *Reflecting a Prairie Town: A Year in Peterson* (Iowa City: University of Iowa Press, 1994), 10.

5. James F. Barber, "Introduction: Order and Image in the American Small Town," *Southern Quarterly* 19:1 (Fall 1980): 3-4.

6. Lawrence W. Farris, "Notes after Nine Years of Small-Town Ministry," *Congregations: The Alban Journal* 24:6 (November-December 1998): 19.

7. Wayne Franklin, Foreword to Richard V. Francaviglia, *Main Street Revisited: Time, Space and Image Building in Small-Town America* (Iowa City: University of Iowa Press, 1996), xi.

8. Hokanson, *Reflecting a Prairie Town,* 166.

9. Hokanson, *Reflecting a Prairie Town*, 69.

10. David Plowden, *Small Town America* (New York: Harry N. Abrams, 1994), 46.

11. Paul Shephard, "Place in American Culture," *North American Review* 262 (1977): 32.

Chapter 2: History

1. Osha Gray Davidson, *Broken Heartland: The Rise of America's Rural Ghetto* (New York: Free Press, 1990), 101ff.

2. See, for example, Hans Bertens and Theo D'Haen, eds., *The Small Town in America: A Multidisciplinary Revisit* (Amsterdam: VU University Press, 1995), especially part II: "Literary Perspectives"; and Martinez-Brawley, *Perspectives on the Small Community,* especially part 2, "The Community in Fiction and the Press."

3. Walter Hobling, "From Main Street to Lake Wobegon," in Bertens and D'Haen, *The Small Town in America,* 103.

4. Hobling, "From Main Street," 104ff.

5. Gary E. Farley, "Culture and Values," in *Discovering the Uniqueness of Rural Communities* (College Station: Rural Social Science by Extension, Texas Agricultural Extension Service, Texas A&M University, 1989), ch. 4, p. 11.

6. Norris, *Dakota*, 81.

7. Fred E. Schroeder, "Local History and Newcomers," *History News* 40:7 (July 1985): 18-19.

8. Norris, *Dakota*, 87.

9. Plowden, *Small Town America*, 28.

10. L. Shannon Jung and Mary A. Agria, *Rural Congregational Studies: A Guide for Good Shepherds* (Nashville: Abingdon, 1997), 65-66.

11. Norris, *Dakota*, 19-20.

12. Allen and Dillman, *Against All Odds,* 172.

Chapter 3: Culture

1. Jung, *Rural Ministry*, 58ff.

2. Hokanson, *Reflecting a Prairie Town,* 166.

3. See David A. Heenan, *The New Corporate Frontier: The Big Move to Small Town, U.S.A.* (New York: McGraw Hill, 1991), a manual on how corporate America can move into small towns, overcome resistance, and prosper.

4. Hokanson, *Reflecting a Prairie Town*, 175.

5. Johnson and Beale, "Rural Rebound," 49.

6. Allen and Dillman, *Against All Odds*, 26-27.

7. Duncan, *Worlds Apart*, 3-53, 74-96.

8. Davidson, *Broken Heartland*, 138.

9. Davidson, *Broken Heartland*, 49-52.

10. Davidson, *Broken Heartland*, 47ff.

11. Davidson, *Broken Heartland*, 73-76.

12. Duncan, *Worlds Apart*, chapters 1 and 2.

13. Gary E. Farley, "Making a Living," in *Discovering the Uniqueness of the Rural Community*, ch. 5, p. 6.

14. Tracy Kidder, *Home Town* (New York: Random House, 1999), 59.

15. Duncan, *Worlds Apart*, chapters 1 and 2.

16. Duncan, *Worlds Apart*, 29-36.

17. Allen and Dillman, *Against All Odds*, 6.

18. Allen and Dillman, *Against All Odds*, 152.

19. Everett Carll Ladd, Jr., *Ideology in America: Change and Response*

in a City, a Suburb, and a Small Town (Ithaca: Cornell University Press, 1969), 145.

20. Martinez-Brawley, *Perspectives on the Small Community*, 205ff.

21. Gary E. Farley, "Leadership and Power," in *Discovering the Uniqueness of the Rural Community*, 6-1ff.

22. Allen and Dillman, *Against All Odds*, 103-122.

23. Farley, "Leadership and Power," 6-2.

24. Hokanson, *Reflecting a Prairie Town*, 72-73.

25. Norris, *Dakota*, 73-74.

26. Martinez-Brawley, *Perspectives on the Small Community*, 12-15.

27. Allen and Dillman, *Against All Odds*, 156.

28. Plowden, *Small Town America*, 37.

29. Duncan, *Worlds Apart*, 205.

30. Farley, "Leadership and Power," 6-3.

31. Farley, "Leadership and Power," 6-3.

32. Allen and Dillman, *Against All Odds*, 153-159.

33. Robert N. Bellah and others, *Habits of the Heart: Individualism and Community in American Life* (Berkeley: University of California Press, 1985), 154.

34. Farris, "Notes after Nine Years," 20.

35. Norris, *Dakota*, 147.

Chapter 4: Values

1. Kidder, *Home Town*, 102.

2. Martinez-Brawley, *Perspectives on the Small Community*, 50.

3. Martinez-Brawley, *Perspectives on the Small Community*, 12.

4. Ralph Keyes, *We the Lonely People: Searching for Community* (New York: Harper & Row, 1973), 145.

5. Plowden, *Small Town America*, 15.

6. Martinez-Brawley, *Perspectives on the Small Community*, 51.

7. Norris, *Dakota,* 72, 74.

8. Martinez-Brawley, *Perspectives on the Small Community*, 39.

9. Farley, "Leadership and Power," ch. 6, p. 8.

10. Kidder, *Home Town*, 69.

11. See Duncan, *Worlds Apart*, chapter 3.

12. Norris, *Dakota,* 56.

13. Farris, "Notes after Nine Years," 19.

14. Norris, *Dakota*, 56.

15. Franklin and Steiner, "Taking Place," 7.

16. Kidder, *Home Town*, 337.

17. Norris, *Dakota*, 57, 61.

18. Kidder, *Home Town*, 91.

19. Norris, *Dakota*, 113.

20. Kidder, *Home Town*, 337.

Chapter 5: Ministerial Role

1. Farris, "Notes after Nine Years," 18.

2. Jane Smiley, *A Thousand Acres* (New York: Alfred A. Knopf, 1991), 210-211.

3. Norris, *Dakota*, 55.

4. Farris, "Notes after Nine Years," 19.

5. Farris, "Notes after Nine Years," 19.

6. Norris, *Dakota*, 111.

7. Jung, *Rural Ministry*, 214ff.

8. Norris, *Dakota*, 49-50.

9. Farris, "Notes after Nine Years," 20.

10. Darold H. Beekman, "Ministry Among the People of the Land in the '80s," *Word and World* 6:1 (Winter 1986): 8.

11. Norris, *Dakota*, 166.

12. Beekman, "Ministry Among the People of the Land," 16-17.

Chapter 6: Pastoral Care

1. Beekman, "Ministry Among the People of the Land," 5; and Raymond T. Coward, "Family Life in Small Towns and Rural Communities: Persistence, Change and Diversity," in Robert Craycroft and Michael Fazio, eds., *Change and Tradition in the American Small Town* (Jackson: University Press of Mississippi, 1983), 73-86.

2. Beekman, "Ministry Among the People of the Land," 9-10.

3. From Deborah Cronin, *Can Your Dog Hunt?* (Lima, Ohio: Fairway Press, 1995), 7, cited in Jung and Agria, *Rural Congregational Studies*, 81.

Chapter 7: Congregational Role and Ministry

1. Gary Goreham, Introduction to Unit 4, "Response of the Rural Church to Social, Economic, and Demographic Change," in *The Rural Church in*

America (College Station: Rural Social Science by Extension, Texas Agricultural Extension Service, Texas A&M University, 1991), ch. 1, p. 2.

2. Gary E. Farley, "Effecting Change" in *Discovering the Uniqueness of Rural Communities*, 7-2, 7-7.

3. Jung, *Rural Ministry*, 118.

4. Allen and Dillman, *Against All Odds*, 167.

5. Norman Wirzba, "Caring and Working: An Agrarian Perspective," *Christian Century*, 166:25 (September 22-29, 1999): 655.

6. Farley, "Effecting Change," 7-3.

7. Jung, *Rural Ministry*, 83.

8. Farley, "Effecting Change," 7-3.

9. An excellent resource in this regard is Gilson A. C. Waldkoenig and William O. Avery, *Cooperating Congregations: Portraits of Mission Strategies* (Bethesda: Alban, 2000).

10. Marshall E. Schirer and Mary Anne Forehand, *Cooperative Ministry: Hope for Small Churches* (Valley Forge: Judson, 1984), 23ff.

11. See, for example, Carl Geores, *Building Your Own Model for Cooperative Ministry: A Bible Study Process* (Louisville: Evangelism and Church Development, National Ministries Division of the Presbyterian Church [U.S.A.], n.d.).

12. Jung, *Rural Ministry*, 176.

13. Schirer and Forehand, *Cooperative Ministry*, 28-29.

14. Jung, *Rural Ministry*, 86.

15. Farley, "Effecting Change," 7-5.

16. Jung, *Rural Ministry*, 77.

17. R. Stephen Warner, *New Wine in Old Wineskins: Evangelicals and Liberals in a Small-Town Church* (Berkeley: University of California Press, 1988).

BIBLIOGRAPHY

Books and Articles

Allen, John C., and Don A. Dillman. *Against All Odds: Rural Community in the Information Age.* Boulder: Westview Press, 1994.

Barber, James F. "Introduction: Order and Image in the American Small Town." *Southern Quarterly* 19:1 (fall 1980): 3-7.

Beekman, Darold H. "Ministry Among People of the Land in the '80s." *Word and World* 6:1 (winter 1986): 5-17.

Bellah, Robert N., and others. *Habits of the Heart: Individualism and Community in American Life.* Berkeley: University of California Press, 1985.

Bertens, Hans, and Theo D'Haen. *The Small Town in America: A Multidisciplinary Revisit.* Amsterdam: VU University Press, 1995.

Carroll, Jackson W., and others, eds. *Handbook for Congregational Studies.* Nashville: Abingdon Press, 1986.

Craycroft, Robert, and Michael Fazio, eds. *Change and Tradition in the American Small Town.* Jackson: University Press of Mississippi, 1983.

Davidson, Osha Gray. *Broken Heartland: The Rise of America's Rural Ghetto.* New York: Free Press, 1990.

Davies, Richard O. *Main Street Blues: The Decline of Small Town America.* Columbus: Ohio State University Press, 1998.

Duncan, Cynthia M. *Worlds Apart: Why Poverty Persists in Rural America.* New Haven: Yale University Press, 1990.

Farley, Gary E., ed. *Discovering the Uniqueness of Rural Communities.* College Station: Rural Social Science by Extension, Texas Agricultural Extension Service, Texas A&M University, 1989.

Farris, Lawrence W. "Notes after Nine Years of Small-Town Ministry."

Congregations: The Alban Journal 24:6 (November-December 1998): 18-20.

Flora, Cornelia Butler, and others. *Rural Communities: Legacy and Change.* Boulder: Westview Press, 1992.

Francaviglia, Richard V. *Main Street Revisited: Time, Space, and Image Building in Small Town America.* Iowa City: University of Iowa Press, 1996.

Franklin, Wayne, and Michael Steiner, eds. *Mapping American Culture.* Iowa City: University of Iowa Press, 1992.

Geores, Carl. *Building Your Own Model for Cooperative Ministry: A Bible Study Process.* Louisville: Evangelism and Church Development, National Ministries Division of the Presbyterian Church (U.S.A.), n.d.

Goreham, Gary A. *The Rural Church in America.* College Station: Rural Social Science by Extension, Texas Agricultural Extension Service, Texas A&M University, 1991.

————. *The Rural Church in America Facilitators' Guide.* College Station: Rural Social Service by Extension, Texas Agricultural Extension Service, Texas A&M University, 1991.

Greene, Melissa Fay. *Praying for Sheetrock.* New York: Fawcett Columbine, 1991.

Haruf, Kent. *Plainsong.* New York: Alfred A. Knopf, 1999.

Heat-Moon, William Least. *Blue Highways: A Journey into America.* Boston: Little, Brown, 1982.

Heenan, David A. *The New Corporate Frontier: The Big Move to Small Town, U.S.A.* New York: McGraw Hill, 1991.

Hinsdale, Mary Ann, and others. *It Comes from the People: Community Development and Local Theology.* Philadelphia: Temple University Press, 1995.

Hokanson, Drake. *Reflecting a Prairie Town: A Year in Peterson.* Iowa City: University of Iowa Press, 1994.

Johnson, Kenneth M., and Calvin L. Beale. "The Rural Rebound Revisited." *American Demographics* 17:7 (July 1995): 46-54.

Jung, L. Shannon, and Mary A. Agria. *Rural Congregational Studies: A Guide for Good Shepherds.* Nashville: Abingdon, 1997.

Jung, L. Shannon, and others. *Rural Ministry: The Shape of the Renewal to Come.* Nashville: Abingdon, 1998.

Karon, Jan. *At Home in Mitford.* New York: Penguin Books, 1994.

Keillor, Garrison. *Lake Wobegon Days.* New York: Viking, 1985.

Kemmis, Daniel. *Community and the Politics of Place.* Norman: University of Oklahoma Press, 1990.

Keyes, Ralph. *We the Lonely People: Searching for Community.* New York: Harper & Row, 1973.

Kidder, Tracy. *Home Town.* New York: Random House, 1999.

Ladd, Everett Carll, Jr. *Ideology in America: Change and Response in a City, a Suburb, and a Small Town.* Ithaca: Cornell University Press, 1969.

Lewis, Sinclair. *Main Street.* New York: Harcourt, Brace & World, 1948.

McCall, Jack. *The Small Town Survival Guide: Help for Changing the Economic Future of Your Town.* New York: William Morrow, 1993.

Martinez-Brawley, Emelia E. *Perspectives on the Small Community: Humanistic Views for Practitioners.* Silver Spring: National Association of Social Workers Press, 1990.

Morganthau, Tom, and others. "America's Small Town Boom." *Newsweek* 98:1 (July 6, 1981): 26-37.

Nelson, Margaret, and Jan Smith. *Working Hard and Making Do: Surviving in Small Town America.* Berkeley: University of California Press, 1999.

Norris, Kathleen. *Dakota: A Spiritual Geography.* New York: Ticknor & Fields, 1993.

Pearson, T. R. *A Short History of a Small Place.* New York: Henry Holt, 1985.

Plowden, David. *Small Town America.* New York: Harry N. Abrams, 1994.

Roueche, Berton. *Special Places: In Search of Small Town America.* Boston: Little Brown, 1982.

Schrier, Marshall E., and Mary Anne Forehand. *Cooperative Ministry: Hope for Small Churches.* Valley Forge: Judson, 1984.

Schroeder, Fred E. H. "Local History and Newcomers." *History News* 40:7 (July 1985): 18-21.

————. "Types of American Small Towns and How to Read Them." *Southern Quarterly* 19:1 (fall 1980): 104-135.

Shephard, Paul. "Place in American Culture." *North American Review* 262:3 (fall 1977): 22-32.

Sim, R. Alex. *Land and Community.* Guelph, Ontario: University of Guelph Press, 1988.

Smiley, Jane. *A Thousand Acres.* New York: Alfred A. Knopf, 1991.

United States Bureau of the Census. *Statistical Abstract of the United States: 1998.* Washington, D.C., 1998.

Vissing, Yvonne Marie. *Out of Sight, Out of Mind: Homeless Children and Families in Small Town America.* Lexington: University of Kentucky Press, 1996.

Waldkoenig, Gilson A. C., and William O. Avery. *Cooperating Congregations: Portraits of Mission Strategies.* Bethesda: Alban, 2000.

Warner, R. Stephen. *New Wine in Old Wineskins.* Berkeley: University of California Press, 1988.

Wirzba, Norman. "Caring and Working: An Agrarian Perspective." *Christian Century* 116:25 (September 22-29, 1999): 898-901.

Web Sites

http://www.ruralchurch.org—to connect with Heartland Network for Town and Rural Ministries, Rural Church Network for Town and Rural Ministries of North America, Town and Rural Resource Program, Town and Country Church Institute (http://www.ltsg.edu/sem/tci_1.htm) and Rural Social Science Education (rsse.tamu.edu).

http://www.ruralministry.com—to connect with the Center for Theology and Land in Dubuque, Iowa.

http://smalltown.sarc.msstate.edu—to connect with the Small Town Center at Mississippi State University.

Films

Many recent films afford accurate insights into the life of small towns. Among the more helpful are:

A River Runs Through It. Robert Redford, director, 1992.
Fried Green Tomatoes. John Avnet, director, 1991.
Hoosiers. David Anspaugh, director, 1986.
Message in a Bottle. Luis Mandoki, director, 1999.
Nobody's Fool. Robert Benton, director, 1994.
Norma Rae. Martin Ritt, director, 1979.
October Sky. Joe Johnston, director, 1999.
Places in the Heart. Robert Benton, director, 1984.
Stand By Me. Rob Reiner, director, 1986.

Steel Magnolias. Herbert Ross, director, 1989.
Tender Mercies. Bruce Beresford, director, 1983.
The Apostle. Robert Duvall, director, 1998.
The Spitfire Grill. Lee David Zlotoff, director, 1996.
The Straight Story. David Lynch, director, 1999.
Varsity Blues. Brian Robbins, director, 1999.
What's Eating Gilbert Grape. Lasse Hallstrom, director, 1993.

Radio

National Public Radio stations continue to carry Garrison Keillor's "A Prairie Home Companion," usually on weekends.